Old Testament Fait

Many people today are curious about the life and faith of the Old Testament. What relevance do its laws and wise sayings have to modern life? What can we learn today from this foundation-document of many societies? As so many today look back to ancient religions, what does it teach us about faith and worship and our relationship with God?

John Drane has already covered the history of Old Testament times in his book *The Old Testament Story*. In this book he grapples with the moral and religious ideas of the Old Testament: the spirituality of the Psalms, the wisdom of Proverbs, the uncompromising faith of the prophets. He shows that New Testament faith has its roots deep in Old Testament religion.

This book is an addition to a series by John Drane which introduces the whole Bible for the non-specialist reader:
- *The Old Testament Story*
- *The Old Testament Faith*
- *Jesus and the Four Gospels*
- *Paul*
- *The Life of the Early Church*

Each of the volumes is backed by photographs, maps, time-charts and diagrams. It is a presentation equally suitable for the general reader as for the school or college examination student. *The Life of the Early Church* was described as 'scholarly and open, lively and clear, lavishly and imaginatively illustrated' (*Catholic Herald*), and *The Old Testament Story* as 'a very successful plain history of Israel which can be commended to anyone looking for a beginner's guide' (*Church Times*).

John Drane is a Lecturer in Religious Studies at Stirling University. He has presented several religious programmes on television in Scotland.

To my father,
and in memory of my mother

OLD TESTAMENT FAITH

An Illustrated Documentary

by John Drane

1817

HARPER & ROW, PUBLISHERS, SAN FRANCISCO
Cambridge, Hagerstown, New York, Philadelphia
London, Mexico City, São Paulo, Singapore, Sydney

Contents

Sources of quotations

The majority of Bible quotations are from the *Good News Bible*, copyright 1966, 1971 and 1976, American Bible Society, published by Bible Societies/ Collins. A small number of quotations are from the *Revised Standard Version*, copyright 1946 and 1952, second edition 1971, Division of Christian Education, National Council of the Churches of Christ in the USA.

Chapter Three

John Calvin, *A Commentary on Genesis*, Banner of Truth, 1965, pp. 79–80 (reprint of the Calvin Translation Society edition, 1847).

D. Baly, *God and History in the Old Testament*, Harper and Row, 1976, p. 123.

Chapter Four

E. Brunner, *The Divine Imperative*, Lutterworth Press, 1937/Westminster Press, 1979, p. 86.

Chapter Six

G. W. Anderson, *A Critical Introduction to the Old Testament*, Duckworth, 1959, p. 118.

G. Von Rad, *Old Testament Theology*, vol. 2, p. 319.

G. Von Rad, in *Essays on Old Testament Hermeneutics* (ed. C. Westermann), John Knox Press, 1963, p. 39.

Law Books

The Pentateuch, five books traditionally associated with Moses, contains accounts of humanity's beginnings (Genesis 1-11), accounts of Israel's forefathers (the rest of Genesis), and accounts of Israel's escape from Egypt and journey to the promised land (parts of Exodus, Numbers and Deuteronomy). But above all it contains 'laws': regulations for religious and social life, and great moral laws built on the Ten Commandments.

GENESIS
EXODUS
LEVITICUS
NUMBERS
DEUTERONOMY

History Books

These books tell the story of the Israelites from their first entry into Canaan until their return there after exile in Babylon. Joshua and Judges are about the conquest and settlement of the land. The Books of Samuel are mainly about Kings Saul and David, and Kings concerns first Solomon and then the kings of the divided kingdoms until the monarchy ended with the exile. Chronicles covers similar ground from a different viewpoint, and is linked to Ezra and Nehemiah and their stories of the returned exiles.

JOSHUA
JUDGES
RUTH
1 SAMUEL
2 SAMUEL
1 KINGS
2 KINGS
1 CHRONICLES
2 CHRONICLES
EZRA
NEHEMIAH
ESTHER

The Old Testament Library

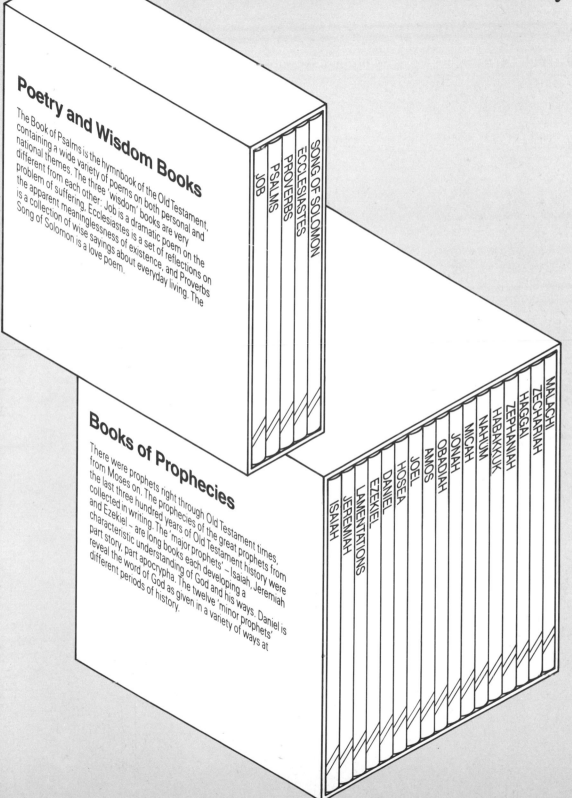

Poetry and Wisdom Books

The Book of Psalms is the hymnbook of the Old Testament, containing a wide variety of poems on both personal and national themes. The three 'wisdom' books are very different from each other: Job is a dramatic poem on the problem of suffering, Ecclesiastes is a set of reflections on the apparent meaninglessness of existence, and Proverbs is a collection of wise sayings about everyday living. The Song of Solomon is a love poem.

JOB · PSALMS · PROVERBS · ECCLESIASTES · SONG OF SOLOMON

Books of Prophecies

There were prophets right through Old Testament times, from Moses on. The prophecies of the great prophets were collected in writing. The 'major prophets' – Isaiah, Jeremiah and Ezekiel – are long books each developing a characteristic understanding of God and his ways. Daniel is part story, part apocrypha. The twelve 'minor prophets' reveal the word of God as given in a variety of ways at different periods of history.

ISAIAH · JEREMIAH · LAMENTATIONS · EZEKIEL · DANIEL · HOSEA · JOEL · AMOS · OBADIAH · JONAH · MICAH · NAHUM · HABAKKUK · ZEPHANIAH · HAGGAI · ZECHARIAH · MALACHI

1 Defining the faith

The story and the faith

OF ALL the literature that has come to us from the world's ancient civilizations, none is as fascinating – or as provocative – as the Old Testament. Some things in it may seem to us either obscure or outmoded, yet it still has an irresistible attraction as one of the world's greatest books. It is, of course, more than just one book. It is a whole library of books – and therein lies its appeal. From the great epic stories of heroes such as Abraham, Moses, Joshua, or David, to the more reflective books such as Job or Ecclesiastes, there is something here for everyone. Enchanting stories of human intrigue and passion stand side by side with philosophical enquiries into the meaning of human life.

Unlikely materials, you may think, from which to construct a coherent collection of literature. But they are perfectly joined together not only by the fact that they are part of a common story. They are also united by a common faith. The Old Testament books are all different, and its leading characters as multifarious as any to be found in the modern world. But in the end they all make sense together because they were all committed to faith in the same God – the God whom they believed had chosen their nation to be a channel of his love to the rest of the world.

Genesis 12:1–3

In the midst of all the diversity that is inevitable in books written over a period of 1000 years and more, the one thing that holds the various elements of the Old Testament together is the fact that God and his activity stand at the centre.

It is, of course, possible to read the Old Testament and never discover its faith. If we think of religious faith as a collection of carefully articulated systematic beliefs about God and how he relates to every conceivable circumstance of human life and thinking, then we are likely to be disappointed by the Old Testament. It certainly contains nothing comparable to a modern book of systematic theology.

So how can we begin to understand the specifically religious dimension of the Old Testament? Where and what is the Old Testament faith? This is one of the more difficult issues for Old Testament scholars today, for a variety of reasons:

● We talk of the Old Testament as if it was a single unified book. But in reality it is a whole library of books, covering the greater part of 1000 years in the history of ancient Israel. These books not only cover a vast time span – they also represent a wide range of literary types. Because of this it is a good deal easier to identify the faith of various Old Testament authors than it is to discover a comprehensive 'Old Testament faith'. Indeed, many scholars believe that the best we can hope for is to speak of 'the faith of the prophets', or 'the faith of the psalmists', and so on.

Opposite
The Old Testament gives us the faith of prophets, lawgivers, kings. But is it possible to discover in its pages the faith to which ordinary children were brought up?

● Is the Old Testament a guide to what people should believe, or is it a record of what people in Israel did as a matter of fact believe? As a book of history, it is both of course. But depending on which one we call 'the Old Testament faith', we will obviously reach rather different conclusions. For example, the prophets declared that true worship of God included the way a person behaves in everyday life,

Amos 5:21–24; Micah 6:6–8; Isaiah 1:10–17

Religion involved every part of life in Old Testament times. The home, the market-place and everyday human relationships were affected as much as affairs of state.

not just ritual actions at a shrine. But both prophets and historians make it perfectly clear that this understanding of worship was not shared by the majority of people in ancient Israel. Similar diversity of opinion can be found on many other issues. So from the outset we need to clarify what we are looking for when we talk of the Old Testament faith. Is it the sort of religious beliefs that were generally held in Israel, or are we trying to extract some system of ideal beliefs out of the Old Testament records?

● Just to complicate things a little more, we also need to remember that both actual practice and the ideals of people such as the prophets changed from one period of Israel's history to another. Take the question of marriage. By the time of Ezra, towards the end of the Old Testament period, it was assumed that one man would marry one woman. But in earlier times it was the common practice for a man to have several wives, and this practice is never explicitly forbidden anywhere in the Old Testament. The same is true of laws governing things such as food, keeping the sabbath day, or circumcision, all of which were a good deal more important after the time of exile in Babylon than they had been before.

Faith, religion and theology

In view of this complexity, some would say there is no such thing as a comprehensive Old Testament faith. On this view, the best we could hope for would be a carefully researched description of the history of

Israelite religion, tracing the ways it developed over many generations.

There is nothing wrong with such an approach. Indeed, given the nature of our material, it is a vital step in the process of discovering the religious faith of the Old Testament writers. When the Old Testament is viewed from the standpoint of the history of religions, it is perhaps the only necessary step. But here we are looking at it as a part of the Christian Bible, not just as religious history, and in this context other questions must be asked. How do the religious ideas of the Old Testament relate to the Christian faith as it can be derived from the New Testament and the teaching of Jesus?

The fact that we are beginning from an undisguised Christian position does not, of course, mean that we can avoid the important historical and literary questions posed by the Old Testament literature. Many such questions have already been dealt with in the companion book to this one, *The Old Testament Story*. The conclusions reached there are simply taken for granted here. Nor does it mean that we wish to despise the work of historians of religion. Without their efforts to elucidate the various developments of the Old Testament faith, we could never get very far. But our Christian stance means we will want to go further, and explore some of the more problematical sections of the Old Testament – its ethics

Israel and Judah could not remain totally detached from the great nations of the Old Testament centuries. King Sargon II of Assyria (right) attacked Judah in the days of Isaiah. An Egyptian worshipper (below) represents a civilization with much influence in the whole area.

A model reconstruction of Solomon's temple. Old Testament religion was national as well as local, centred on the holy city of Jerusalem.

and sacrificial worship, for example – and ask what they are actually saying about God's nature and about true religious belief and practice.

We shall return to these questions in our final chapter. But first we must set the Old Testament faith in its proper social and historical context. Once we have done that we will be in a better position to understand the issues, and hopefully come to some sensible conclusions.

2 The living God

Who is God?

THE QUESTION 'Who is God?' is as old as the human race itself. Philosophers and theologians, as well as countless multitudes of ordinary people down through the ages, have tried to find an answer to it. To some, God is a kind of invisible 'force' who keeps things ticking over smoothly. They may even think of him in the same terms as 'the laws of nature'. To others, God is associated with the various features of the natural world, such as the sun or moon, trees or rocks. Yet others suggest that since the most significant aspect of existence is the human personality itself, then God must be found in the depths of human experience. There are also many others who claim that to talk of God at all is quite irrelevant. Human life, the atheist believes, is complete in itself. It may not always make sense, but there is nothing more to existence than what we can feel and see and handle.

The Old Testament deals with the question in a completely different way. Its answer is clear and straightforward. Far from arguing about God's existence, it simply takes him for granted. We will look in vain to find in the Old Testament any real discussion of the case put forward by the atheist. To be sure, the Old Testament expresses many searching questions about God's reality and his activity. It contains at least one book which never mentions his name (Esther), and another which puts a serious question mark against his concern for the world and its inhabitants (Ecclesiastes). But even these books assume that God is there, and their questionings and probings are carried out in the context of a community which was well aware of the reality of the God whom it worshipped.

The actual statements made about God vary from one Old Testament book to another. New opportunities and fresh experiences of life pose new questions about many aspects of God's being and activity. In the 'Song of Moses', an ancient poem celebrating God's greatness and goodness to his people Israel, we find this rhetorical question: 'Lord, who among the gods is like you? Who is like you, wonderful in holiness? Who can work miracles and mighty acts like yours?' The implied answer, of course, is 'No one', and the poem ends with a commitment that 'You, Lord, will be king for ever and ever'. Even at this early period in Israel's experience, they were certain that their God was more powerful than any other, and so they must give him their undivided allegiance. They did not stop to ask whether other so-called 'gods' really existed. That was hardly necessary, for they knew in their own lives the reality and power of their own God.

The changing fortunes of their nation over the next 700 years, however, brought that question into clearer focus. In the face of great national disaster, some wanted to suggest that Israel's exclusive worship of just one God had contributed to their decline. But, taking their inspiration from the great prophets who had preceded them, the Old Testament history writers were convinced that this was quite wrong. Far from allowing the events of Israel's history to turn them away from the exclusive worship of their own God, they categorically denied that any other gods really could exist. The God of Israel was

Exodus 15:11

Exodus 15:18

Opposite
The Old Testament people had no doubt God existed. But they had the same questions as people everywhere and always: What is God like? How does he affect our lives?

not one God among others – not even the most powerful. He was, in the words of a later Old Testament prophet, 'the first, the last, the only God; there is no other god but me'.

Isaiah 44:6

Although the details of Old Testament beliefs about God were redrawn from time to time, the whole picture is consistent and quite clear in its main outlines. The God of whom it speaks is an all-powerful God, whose concern extends not only to the world of creation, but also to the events of history and to the lives of individual people.

Three things in particular distinguish Old Testament beliefs about God from other ideas current in the world of ancient Israel.

God is invisible

Every nation with which Israel came into contact depicted its gods and goddesses in the shape of idols. They frequently portrayed them as animals. The native religion of the land of Canaan, which was often so attractive to Israel, generally portrayed its god Baal in the form of a young bull, the symbol of life and sexual virility. The Egyptians also used this, and other symbols, to represent their gods. Right from the start, Israel was under constant pressure to do the same.

Exodus 32:1–35; Deuteronomy 9:7–21

While Moses was on Mt Sinai receiving the Law, his people were down below melting their gold jewellery to make a calf which they could worship! Idol-worship became an especially pressing problem after the once-proud empire of David and Solomon had disintegrated to become the two states of Israel and Judah. At that time, the creation of two national shrines became a political as well as a religious necessity. King Jeroboam of Israel gave religious backing to his political stance by erecting golden bulls at the northern sanctuaries of Bethel and Dan. He could see good reasons for doing this. Some of his subjects were not Israelites at all, but Canaanites, and what better way of gaining their support than by erecting religious images to represent their favourite god, Baal? And since the Israelites had long been familiar with the ark of the covenant – a portable 'holy box' giving visible form to the invisible presence of God – why could they not think of the bulls in the same way? But however sophisticated Jeroboam's reasoning, he received the unbridled condemnation of the Old Testament history writers for his actions. Whether he had intended it or not, his people worshipped these bulls as idols, and Jeroboam went down in history as the king who had 'led the people of Israel into sin'.

1 Kings 12:28–33

1 Kings 14:1–16

It was a serious mistake to create any kind of statue that could be worshipped as a god. The belief that God is invisible is firmly embedded in every strand of the Old Testament. Idols are prohibited in the second of the Ten Commandments, and the book of Isaiah contains one of the most sophisticated condemnations of idolatry to be found in any literature anywhere.

Exodus 20:4–5; Deuteronomy 5:8–9

Isaiah 44:9–20

God is not a natural force

Most of the religions of the ancient Near East were means of explaining and controlling the world of nature as it affected the lives of men and women. In Egypt, the annual flooding of the Nile was essential to the well-being of its people. Much Egyptian religion was therefore concerned to ensure that this would continue. Elsewhere in the Fertile Crescent, the fertility of fields and flocks was bound up with the appearance of the rains at the right time of year. This was the case in Canaan, the land in which the people of Israel settled after their dramatic escape from slavery in Egypt. The Ras Shamra texts, found at the site of the ancient city of Ugarit, have shed much light on the religion of the Canaanites at the time when the Israelites settled in their new land. They contain stories about the doings of various gods and goddesses – El, Anat, Baal and others. Many features of the stories are unclear, but it is obvious that the activities of the gods personify the cycle of the seasons. For instance, the story of how Baal dies, and is returned to life by the sexual attentions of his lover Anat, has close connexions with the apparent death and rebirth of the life of nature that took place year by year as one season succeeded another.

The people of Israel were often tempted to worship Baal instead of their own God. For this the Old Testament condemns them roundly. By so doing they misunderstood the character of God in a fundamental way. He is above nature, not a part of nature. And though he can on occasion be described in imagery derived from natural phenomena such as light or fire, he can never be identified with the forces of the natural world.

Psalm 104:2; Ezekiel 1:27–28
Exodus 19:18; Deuteronomy 4:32, 36

God is not an abstraction

Canaanite religion centred on worship of Baal, god of fertility, sometimes portrayed as a young bull. Resheph, seen in the statue below, was a god of plague and disasters.

The Old Testament never tries to define God. In one sense this is hardly surprising, for if God is greater than the sum of human intelligence then he must be beyond description. But that has not generally prevented people from making the effort. In the early Christian centuries readers of the Bible spent much time and energy trying to decide how to describe God. Modern books of systematic theology often begin in the same way, by trying to define God's being

Greek philosophers, such as Plato, speculated about God's being. The Hebrews were interested in how to relate to God.

in abstract terms – almost as if there is some chemical or mathematical formula that, if only we can find it, will give us access to the innermost depths of his existence.

This approach has a long and venerable history going back at least to the work of the great Greek philosophers. They tried to explain God in an abstract, or metaphysical, way. To answer the question 'Who is God?' it was therefore necessary to ask a further question, 'What is God made of?' This is not the way the Old Testament thinks about God. Its writers do not try to analyze God as if he was a specimen under a microscope. The world of abstract thought is quite foreign to their concept of God. Instead of defining God metaphysically, by asking what he is made of, they defined him functionally, by exploring his relevance to human life and experience. They were asking the same questions as the modern theologian or philosopher, but they took a very different route to get to the answer.

A simple example will explain the difference. If someone asks me to describe my lover I can give two rather different answers. I can describe her appearance – height, weight, colour of hair, colour of eyes, and so on. This would certainly answer the question, and it would allow the questioner to form a mental picture of her appearance. But it would also leave many things unanswered, and if the questioner really wanted to get to know and understand my partner, it would be an altogether unsatisfactory sort of answer. A more useful answer would include some description of the kind of person that she is, illustrated with personal anecdotes to show how she has reacted to life in particular circumstances. To give that sort of answer I need never mention things like the colour of her hair, and I might well refer to undefinable notions such as 'love' as the key to her personality. The philosopher would find great difficulty with all that, but most people would accept this rather emotive description of my partner as a good deal more helpful than a series of abstract observations about her external appearance.

This is how the Old Testament speaks about God. It answers the question 'Who is God?' by laying all the emphasis on the way he relates to the world and its people. It never analyzes him in an abstract, factual kind of way.

What is God like?

In one sense, the entire Old Testament is the answer to this question. As we read its books we can see how they are all concerned to describe the different ways in which God has revealed himself to his people. At the very beginning of Genesis we have a series of ancient stories that tell how God relates to the world of creation. These are followed by the long and complex accounts of his dealings with the nation of Israel from the time of Abraham in the Middle Bronze Age (2000-1500 BC) right through to the time of the Persian Empire and beyond, just a century or two before Christ. Then in addition to God's revelation through nature and history, the Old Testament contains many books showing how God relates to the

One way God has shown himself to humanity is in the world he created. The beginning of Genesis says repeatedly of the creation that 'it was good'.

more mundane circumstances of everyday life – either the corporate life of society or the personal spiritual experience of individuals. With such variety in its literature the Old Testament contains many different perspectives on the involvement of God with his people. But some themes are so common that they are obviously fundamental to the total Old Testament picture of God.

An active God   The Old Testament is distinguished from most other religious books by its great emphasis on the facts of history. The messages of the prophets, as well as the history books, declare that God is to be encountered in the varied events of Israel's national life. Other nations in the world of ancient Israel sometimes thought of their gods as being involved in political life. But what distinguishes the Old Testament is that God's activity is seen not in isolated incidents, but throughout the whole story. Indeed, it is only because God is at work there that the history has a coherent meaning at all.

Scholars of a previous generation often saw this as the main key to understanding the Old Testament. They laid all the emphasis on the notion of a 'God who acts'. This is perhaps too simplistic a way of describing the Old Testament faith, for some of its books scarcely mention God's actions in Israel's history. But there can be no doubt that this is one of its more distinctive features. Life is not just a meaningless cycle of empty existence. It has a beginning and an end, and events happen not in a haphazard sequence but as part of a great design that in turn is based on the character of God himself. And this God is encountered by his people in the ordinary events of everyday life, and not through tortuous intellectual debate.

This confident assertion dominates the Old Testament story. From the early accounts of the call of Abraham, right through to the apocalyptic visions of the book of Daniel, it is God who is in control of history. In bad times as well as good, all that happens is part of God's plan for his people. Because of this overriding conviction, the way the Old Testament writers tell the story of their people is quite different from the approach of the modern historian. A modern reader may look for historical explanations of a particular event, assuming that if history makes sense at all it is a sense that comes from within itself rather than depending on the external influence of God.

It is, of course, possible to read the Old Testament in this way, and to some extent we have done so in the companion volume, *The Old Testament Story*. But if we restrict our thinking to historical cause and effect we will miss an important dimension of what the Old Testament writers were saying.

● **God chooses his people** Their story begins with Abraham, a pagan merchant who leaves his homeland in Mesopotamia and heads west and south to make a new life for himself. Abraham's journey was, in fact, typical of many such journeys that were being made in the Middle Bronze Age (2000-1500 BC). People were

This standard was found in the city of Ur, on the River Euphrates, from which Abram set out in faith.

moving in all directions through the Fertile Crescent, and Abraham was certainly not alone in making the journey from east to west in search of a new way of life. But this is not important to the Old Testament. Abraham's migration was not just a symptom of demographic changes: it was an integral part of God's plan for his life. Not only was he to have a new lifestyle: he was also to become the ancestor of a great nation. Through him God would 'bless all the nations'. The driving force in Abraham's life – as in that of his successors – was the intention of a loving and all-powerful God to share his love with the whole world and its people.

Genesis 12:3

This belief found its classical expression in the story of how a group of Abraham's descendants were released from slavery in Egypt (the exodus). This is the heart of the Old Testament faith. For centuries afterwards the people of Israel looked back to this event to remind them of God's goodness and their responsibilities. Here again, it may well be that various details of the exodus story can be explained by reference to features of the geography or natural history of the area. But this is not the way the Old Testament describes it. For Israel, it was more than just a story. The dramatic escape from slavery and their settlement in the land of Canaan was due not to social or geographical factors. It was the action of God himself. Without his intervention it could never have taken place.

When later generations wanted to remind themselves of the character of their God, they turned to the exodus story. This event

The Assyrian army, seen here using a siege-engine and battering-ram to attack a city, was a formidable force. Yet the prophet Isaiah could assure the people of Jerusalem that God would protect them from Assyrian invasion.

Archaeologists believe they may have found remains of the wall Nehemiah persuaded the exiles to rebuild when they returned to Jerusalem. This leader took all his decisions in the context of prayer to God who was personally concerned for his people.

was celebrated in poetry and in song, and reported in family groups at every opportunity. It became the central focus of their faith. Not only did it remind them that God was active in history: it also gave a unique insight into the nature of that activity – and therefore into the character of God himself.

● **God's love** is a major theme that runs through the whole story. The slaves were powerless and weak. Even their leaders were uncertain of the future, and had the nation depended for its survival on human ingenuity and courage, then it would have failed. When later generations celebrated this great event, God's generous actions towards his people (his 'grace') were always in the centre of their thoughts. An ancient creed, recited as the first-fruits of later harvests were offered, puts it like this: 'We cried out for help to the Lord, the God of our ancestors. He heard us and saw our suffering, hardship and misery. By his great power and strength he rescued us from Egypt ...' This theme was given a powerful social dimension by the prophets to remind the people that God has a particular care for those who are the victims of unjust oppression. The exodus was not just a demonstration of God's powerful actions in history: it was also an experience of his love, which found its truest fulfilment when it centred on those who were past helping themselves.

Deuteronomy 26:7–8

● **God's power** over the whole of life is another dominant theme in the exodus story. God acts not only in the lives of his people to bring about their salvation: he also controls the powers of nature itself. He meets Moses in the burning bush; he sends the plagues on the Egyptians; he parts the Sea of Reeds – and later the River Jordan – to allow the escaping slaves to cross on dry land. He provides food and water in the course of the long desert journey – even flocks of birds can be sent at his command to feed those who are hungry. Nations are also in his control. Both Egyptians and Canaanites are used by God to accomplish his purposes. Sometimes they become instruments of judgment, at others of blessing – but always as part of God's loving purpose for his people.

Exodus 3:1–10
Exodus 7:14 — 11:9
Exodus 14:1–31; Joshua 3:1–17

Exodus 15:22 — 17:7

● **God's justice** is a prominent element in the story of the exodus. At the heart of the story we find the Old Testament Law, the *Torah*. It is significant that this is an integral part of the story of God's actions on behalf of his people. At the heart of the Old Testament faith is the belief that God acts in accordance with his own clearly defined standards of justice – never in an arbitrary or unpredictable fashion. The core of God's relationship with his people is morality and when a person encounters God it is always in the context of moral challenge. When Isaiah had a vision of God in the temple, it was not the other-worldly, supernatural aspects of the experience that impressed him; his first response was to confess his own inadequacy in the face of the great moral purity of God. When God reveals himself, whether in temple or in exodus, his people must face up to the demands of his justice.

Isaiah 6:1–5

● **Finding God in later history** These three features of God's activity dominate the rest of the Old Testament story. It was in the process of trying to relate God's love, power and justice that the prophets hammered out some of the most distinctive elements of the Old Testament faith. As time went on, it became increasingly clear that Israel's fortunes were closely connected to the international power politics of the day. Israel and Judah were just pawns in the strategic manoeuvres of the two superpowers based in Egypt and Mesopotamia who vied with each other for domination of the Fertile Crescent. It often seemed as if these powers were in control of things, not God. What then was the value of God's promises – not only his promise to Abraham and his mighty acts in the exodus, but his bold assurance to David that 'I will make you as famous as the greatest leaders in the world ... You will always have descendants and I will make your kingdom last for ever. Your dynasty will never end'?

2 Samuel 7: 8–16

Viewed in this light, the facts of history raised many awkward questions. If Israel had been chosen by God, should they not be triumphant in all their battles? And if God was in control of things, why should other nations be able to get the upper hand? The prophets had a clear answer to these questions. The fact that God had revealed himself to Israel, showing his love in so many ways, imposed great responsibilities. As Israel were faithful to their calling, so they would prosper. But when they were unfaithful, then they needed to return and ask God's forgiveness. The misfortunes they suffered were a reminder of that. This is how the author of the book of Judges assessed Israel's early history. It was a lesson that the prophets hammered home in many a crisis of the nation's later life.

The people often misunderstood the nature of God's involvement in their history. They imagined that his dealings with them were a sign that they were God's favourites. But the prophets knew that God's purposes were never so restricted. His intention was firm and clear: the salvation of all peoples, as he promised to Abraham. And though Israel had been the special recipient of God's love, and had witnessed his great acts of power, both love and power could only operate within the framework of God's justice.

This conviction often brought the prophets into direct conflict

Following pages
Much like nomadic peoples today, the Israelites retained a sense of being together before God – the group or the nation mattered every bit as much as each individual person.

with the politicians of their day. And they did not always take the same side. Isaiah, for example, could advise the king in Jerusalem that God would protect his city and all would be well in the face of an Assyrian invasion. But a few generations later, Jeremiah said exactly the opposite. What united them was the knowledge that history was in God's control, and he was ordering things in accordance with his own absolute standards. Those who arrogantly set themselves up against him – whether Assyria or Judah herself – would be judged. And when the Babylonians took the king of Judah off into exile and later destroyed the city of Jerusalem, that was as much the work of God as the exodus itself had been.

Isaiah 31:4–5
Jeremiah 7:1–15

Jeremiah 24

Many people found that hard to understand. After all, their entire history seemed to suggest that God was on their side. And if he was, how could he allow a catastrophe such as the exile to befall them? It was at this time that Israel's historians compiled the story of their nation as we now have it in the Old Testament. The Deuteronomistic History, stretching from Deuteronomy to 2 Kings, retold the familiar stories in an effort to explain why God had apparently deserted his people. Following the prophets, it declares that Israel had been disobedient. They had failed in their God-given responsibilities, and had suffered the inevitable consequences. Others compiled the story of Israel's earlier experiences, from creation to the exodus. And they too had a message for their people: disobedience had been a part of human life from the very beginning. But it was always balanced by God's grace and forgiveness. God's justice and God's love could not be separated. And whereas the Deuteronomistic History had a sad and depressing tale to tell, the message from Genesis to Numbers was more encouraging, assuring those in exile that God's love would ultimately triumph.

But what about God's power? Had not the final days of Judah been in effect a battle not between two armies but between two gods – and had not the gods of Babylon won? Where did the God of Israel stand in relation to the apparent power of other gods? This question had been faced in a practical way right from the earliest days, when the tribes had decided to worship only one God. But they had not denied that other gods might exist. Indeed, the eagerness with which they often worshipped Baal suggests that some of them were not at all convinced that their own God was all-powerful.

Joshua 24:1–28

Psalm 47
Amos 1:3 — 2:5

Some of the earlier psalms, as well as prophetic messages from the time of Amos, had hinted that God was in control of the lives of people everywhere, and not of only Israel's destiny. But with the exile the question had become ever more urgent. And it was given a very clear answer in some of the most remarkable passages anywhere in the Old Testament. In a series of prophetic messages, the God of Israel is declared to be the God of the whole world. He is all-powerful, and those who worship other gods are not only misguided but stupid. Far from being a sign of God's defeat, the exile had itself been God's punishment for his people. He had used the Babylonians to do his will, but they too had been punished for their excessive violence. God's power was in no way diminished, and

Isaiah 44:1–20

Isaiah 47:1–15

Isaiah 45:1–4

he would raise up a new deliverer for his people – this time, not a Moses from among them, but Cyrus, the emperor of Persia. The future would be even greater than the past had been, as God would move in a new way to fulfil the original intention of his promise to Abraham. God's servant, through whom this would be accomplished, would bring blessing to Israel, but he would also be 'a light

Isaiah 49:6

to the nations – so that all the world may be saved'.

A personal God

The fact that God reveals his character in the great sweep of history may lead us to wonder if he was not just a personification of 'fate', or even of 'history' itself. Many gods and goddesses of the ancient world were personifications of various aspects of the world of nature. Could it not be that the God of the Old Testament was just a personification of Israel's history?

Things are not quite as simple as that. To the Canaanites, for instance, the world of nature seemed to go its own way regardless of human interest, and there was very little anyone could do to change things. The best one could hope for was to escape the most vindictive aspects of nature by avoiding too much personal involvement with the gods who control it. The Old Testament accepts that God is to be given the honour that is due to him, and recognizes that his ways are often beyond human understanding. But it also emphasizes that he does not relate to people in a purely mechanical way. Quite the opposite. He is intimately interested in both the world and its inhabitants, not remote from people and their needs. All the great events of the Old Testament stress that God does not act in a capricious, unpredictable way. He is not concerned to manipulate events for his own advantage. He is concerned for people and their good. Even more striking is the way he expresses his love. For it is not the patronizing care of a moralist who knows what is best, and is prepared to ride roughshod over human need in order to achieve his ends. Some of the most striking, and unexpected, stories in the Old Testament depict God entering into discussion with his people, and

Genesis 18:16–33; Amos 7:1–6

even changing his mind as a result. We may find all this a little difficult to understand. But it explains why morality and justice are so fundamental to the Old Testament view of God. For it is in the context of personal relationships that such qualities are most important.

● **The individual and society** How then does God relate to his people? There is no doubt that the Old Testament lays much emphasis on the fact that he relates to Israel as a nation. When the tribes escaping from Egypt arrived at Mt Sinai, it was only Moses who went up the mountain to receive God's laws. In that sense, it was only one person who had a direct encounter with God himself. Yet what happened there was not something private and personal: it was a representative experience in which all the people were included. The idea that one person could represent a whole nation in this way was widely held in the ancient world, where kings could be the very embodiment of their nation. The term 'corporate personality' is sometimes used to describe this sense of national solidarity, though it is not a term used by the Old Testament itself and its importance has often been exaggerated.

But it does draw attention to an aspect of Old Testament thinking that is sometimes difficult for modern Western people to grasp. Most of us are accustomed to thinking in terms of the work of an individual – and when we talk of 'society', we mean just the sum total of individuals living in a particular time and place. The Old Testament knows nothing of this kind of narrow individualism. The family, the village, the tribe and the nation were all of crucial importance. A person found fulfilment in life as he or she was in the proper relationship with others. Both happiness and misery were shared with other people, and a sense of social solidarity runs deep in the Old Testament, just as it does in many Asian cultures today. We find this most strikingly in the story of Achan, whose entire tribe was implicated in the sin of just one man. There were clearly risks involved in being closely identified with others! But compared to the fear of being alone, such risks were very small. To have no friends, and to be an outcast, was the final indignity that an Israelite could suffer, for life only found its fullest meaning when a person was a part of society.

Joshua 7:1–26

Jeremiah 15:17; Psalm 102:6–7

It was once fashionable to suppose that people of Old Testament times could see no meaning or purpose in life except as part of a large social unit. But this is to press the idea of corporate personality to a logical conclusion that is never drawn in the Old Testament itself. We would be quite mistaken to imagine that God only deals with people in large numbers. The book of Psalms is an anthology of materials used in the worship of God over generations, and it contains many examples of prayers and hymns which show just how much worshippers in ancient Israel felt that God was personally interested in the details of their own everyday life. The prophets also stressed the importance of individual commitment to the God who revealed himself through the events of their national heritage.

The same theme is prominent in many of the Old Testament's best-known stories. God is personally concerned for the welfare of Abraham and his wife when they find themselves in a hostile land. Later, he takes care of Joseph, saving him first from the jealousy of his brothers and then from the plots of the Egyptians. Nor is his personal interest restricted only to members of the nation of Israel. It extends to the boy Ishmael who, with his mother Hagar, is expelled from Abraham's family circle. Much later in the Old Testament, God's pity covers not only the innocent children of the great city of Nineveh but even the suffering animals in it.

Genesis 12:10–20

Genesis 37:39–41

Genesis 21:9–21

Jonah 4:11

● **Describing God** The importance of recognizing God as a person comes out clearly in much of the imagery that the Old Testament uses to describe him. The messages of the prophet Hosea apply the terminology of personal relationships to God and his people in a particularly sensitive way. God is a loving father to his people, who cared for them and directed their footsteps from the very beginning of their national history. He not only guided them, he also cared for them: 'I drew them to me with affection and love. I

Opposite
The love of God for Israel is sometimes likened to a parent's love for a child.

Hosea 11:4

Exodus 4:22

Isaiah 1:2

Hosea 2:14–23; Jeremiah 31:32

Ezekiel 16:3–8

Isaiah 49:15; 66:13

1 Samuel 4:1–4; Psalm 24

picked them up and held them to my cheek; I bent down to them and fed them.' According to the book of Exodus, this was the message that Moses had given to the pharaoh of Egypt when he reminded him that Israel was God's 'first-born son. I told you to let my son go, so that he might worship me ...' And centuries later, Isaiah depicts God as a broken-hearted father whose children have rejected his guidance.

At other times God can be depicted as the husband of his people. After the fall of Jerusalem Ezekiel portrays him as a generous stepfather who had rescued the city and its people from certain death. Other prophets of the same generation boldly applied the imagery of motherhood to God's love for his people.

In spite of statements such as these, many people feel that the Old Testament picture of God is unsatisfactory and primitive, and especially that it is radically different from the Christian New Testament. This is a misconception of the teaching of both parts of the Christian Bible. God's love for his people and his concern for them in the dangers and difficulties of life was as fundamental to the Old Testament faith as it is to the life and teaching of Jesus.

At the same time, we must not hide the distinctive elements of the Old Testament picture of God. For although it occasionally describes God in terms of close personal and family relationships, it more often portrays him as the ruler, master and lord of his people. He is their sovereign, often in a very literal way. In some early narratives, God leads his people into battle as their army commander ('the Lord of hosts'), his invisible presence symbolized by the ark of the covenant. And though from the time of Saul onwards a human king plays a leading role in the affairs of the people, there is still a considerable emphasis on the fact that God himself is Israel's only true king. Indeed, the Old Testament historians pass their verdict on the various kings of Israel and Judah mainly in relation to whether they have been prepared to recognize the greater kingship of God himself.

Even when the idea of kingship is not explicitly mentioned, much of the imagery used in speaking of God comes from such a background. The well-known Psalm 23 refers to God as the 'shepherd' of his people. To us this suggests a different background of thought. But in the ancient world the king was often referred to as the 'shepherd', and this is almost certainly what the psalmist had in mind.

● **The king and his people** It was perfectly natural for the Old Testament writers to think of God as their king. In rescuing the slaves from Egypt, God had done for them what any good king would do for his people. Many scholars believe that the form in which God's relationship with his people was celebrated (the covenant) owes something to the way in which a subject nation would define its relationship to a greater power that had delivered it from an enemy. Israel's allegiance to God as king was the grateful obedience of those who have been set free, not the fear of those who have been defeated.

If God is the king, then human relationships with him must

Right from the time when he rescued Israel from Egypt, God acted towards his people as a good king to his subjects.

Psalm 113:1; 123:2

Psalm 19:9

naturally be described in terms of obedience and service. God's people are his 'servants', and their attitude towards him is often described as 'fear'. Sometimes the 'fear of the Lord' is just a name for religious worship. But more often it indicates an attitude of mind which recognizes the difference between God and people. We might talk of 'reverence' or 'honour' rather than 'fear', and this is how many modern versions of the Old Testament translate the word. To fear God in this sense has little connexion with popular pictures of an angry God before whom men and women can only cower in insignificance. It is rather a matter of giving God his appropriate place. The importance of recognizing that God is so much greater than men and women is a common Old Testament theme. Even the prophets, who claim to have access to God's innermost secrets and to be on close personal terms with God, nevertheless display a strong sense of awe and reverence as they stand in his presence and hear his word.

No doubt there are many reasons why the Old Testament most often describes God in terms of the king/subject or master/slave imagery. But there was one particularly strong reason for avoiding the language of the family. For much of the Old Testament story Israel was resisting the inroads of Canaanite religion, which laid great stress on the physical relationships of its deities. Gods and goddesses could be portrayed as fathers, sons, mothers, and lovers. They were all related in some way or another, and physical characteristics were an important part of such relationships. The key to unlock life's mysteries could be found in the sexual relationships of gods and goddesses. There was always a strong temptation for

Hosea 2:16

Israel to think of her own God like this. But to talk exclusively of God as 'father' or 'husband' in that context could have suggested little more than a merely physical relationship. It is not surprising therefore that, with one or two striking exceptions, most of the references to God as 'father' are found in the later Old Testament books, coming from an age when the battles with Canaanite religion had receded into the past.

We must remember that all these images are attempts to describe a person who is essentially indescribable. They help to portray some of his characteristics but must all be understood by reference to their broader context. Emphasizing some aspects of the picture at the expense of others leads to distortions. By concentrating on the descriptions of God as a father or husband and his people as children or wife it is easy to miss the sense of reverence and wonder that pervades the Old Testament. But to dwell exclusively on the picture of God as a master and his people as servants is just as misleading if it suggests that he is a harsh, cruel and unpredictable tyrant. The Old Testament recognizes that God is different from men and women. But it declares that the gap between God's perfect being and the imperfect world of humanity is bridged by God's loving actions in saving and blessing. And these actions find their ultimate meaning in the fact that God is not just a force or an abstract will, but a person – with all that that involves.

God's name

The fact that God is a person comes out in the way the Old Testament emphasizes his name. Only people have names, and in the ancient world a person's name was more than just a label.

● A person's name established a person's identity, and revealed their character. So, for example, in the early stories of the book of Genesis, Eve (3:20), Cain (4:1), and Noah (5:29) are all given names that indicate something about their personalities. Later, all twelve ancestors of the Israelite tribes have names that reflect either the nature of the recipients or the experiences of their parents (Genesis 29:31–30:24).

● Knowing a person's name, or giving a name to someone, is often a way of gaining authority over that person. God himself gives the stars their names because he is their Creator (Psalm 147:4). He gives Israel their name, and in doing so asserts his authority over them (Isaiah 43:1). Similarly, when Jacob wrestles with an unknown deity, he wants to know his name so that he may establish a proper relationship with him (Genesis 32:29–30). To know the name of a god could therefore be very important, for a god's name gave the worshipper access to his power. By calling a god's name, his presence could be assured.

The Old Testament attitude to God's name is distinctive. Using God's name in this semi-magical way is expressly forbidden in the Ten Commandments (Exodus 20:7). God's name is not something to be discovered and manipulated by men and women: it is something that God himself reveals in his love to his own people.

What is God's name?

Because of this, there is an extraordinary reverence for God's name throughout the Old Testament. The reticence to mention the name of God is so widespread that we do not even know for certain how his personal name was pronounced. Hebrew has no vowels, and this name was written down as YHWH. Vowel sounds are needed to pronounce it, of course, but we do not know precisely which sounds were used. When the Old Testament was written down in its present form, Jewish religious teachers regarded the personal name of God as too sacred to say. Whenever they found it they would substitute the Hebrew word *Adonai*, which means 'my lord'. In this way, the vowels of *Adonai* came to be pronounced with the consonants of God's name YHWH, to produce something like the English term 'Jehovah'. Nowadays it is customary to write this name as 'Yahweh', and this is the form we have used here.

It is often supposed that this avoidance of God's personal name was a relatively late development in Judaism. But we can find traces of it throughout the Old Testament. For example, in the stories of Joseph, God's name Yahweh is never found on the lips of non-Israelites (Genesis 37–50), and there is a whole section of the book of Psalms which avoids it (Psalms 42–83). Other parts of the Old Testament use the expression 'the Name', instead of speaking directly of God himself (for example Psalm 5:11; 7:17; 9:2, 10; 18:49). This usage is taken up in a particularly constructive way in Deuteronomy, where it is God's 'Name' that is bestowed on the temple in Jerusalem to signify God's presence and blessing there (Deuteronomy 12:11; 14:23, and so on). By having 'the Name', and not Yahweh himself, dwell in the temple, the Old Testament avoids the idea that God was restricted to just one locality, and yet still assures the people that he could be found in the context of worship at Jerusalem.

What does Yahweh mean?

From a purely linguistic point of view, a number of suggestions can be made. The word Yahweh could, for example, be related to an Arabic word meaning 'blow'. Some scholars have argued from this that Yahweh was therefore originally the name of a storm god. Others have suggested that the clue to its meaning is to be found in a shortened form of the name, Ya'u, which is known in Babylon and other parts of the ancient world. Or perhaps it was originally just a shout of excitement used in the context of religious worship, which was subsequently taken as a proper name.

Suggestions such as these are of little use for our purposes here. Explaining where a name comes from is not the same as explaining what it means. And the Old Testament gives a quite distinctive meaning to it. When Moses asks on whose authority he is to go and demand the release of the slaves from Egypt, he is told: 'I am who I am. This is what you must say to them: "The one who is called I AM has sent me to you"' (Exodus 3:14). Even this is not absolutely clear. Several centuries later, when the Old Testament was translated into Greek (the *Septuagint*), this phrase was taken as an indication of God's eternal existence, along the lines of Greek philosophical speculation about God. But it is obvious in the context that, although the name Yahweh is related to the Hebrew verb 'to be', all the emphasis is on God's activity rather than on his existence as such. It is, like the rest of the Old Testament story, a declaration that God is characterized by his actions. His name indicated his nature, and with it came the assurance to the slaves in Egypt that God was active on their behalf. He was the Lord of time itself, and what he had done in the past, he was doing in the present – and would continue to do in the future.

Descriptions of God

As well as the many words, names and titles used for God in the Old Testament, the writers employ numerous evocative images to describe him. These are sometimes missed in the newer translations. Some of the best known are:

Revised Standard Version	Key Reference	Good News Bible
Rock	Deuteronomy 32:4	Mighty defender
Shepherd	Psalm 23:1	Shepherd
Shield	Psalm 18:2	Shield, or sometimes protector
Light	Psalm 27:1	Light
Strength	Psalm 28:7	...protects me
Refuge	Psalm 46:1	Shelter
Sun	Psalm 84:11	Glorious king
Father	Psalm 89:26	Father
Help	Psalm 115:9	Help
Shade	Psalm 121:5	...protects
Song	Isaiah 12:2	(doesn't translate)
Redeemer	Isaiah 41:14	The one who saves you
Husband	Isaiah 54:5	Husband
Fountain	Jeremiah 2:13	Spring
Dew	Hosea 14:5	Rain

This detail from an ancient scroll of Isaiah shows important alterations, from 'adonai' to 'Yahweh' in one case and from 'Yahweh' to 'adonai' in the other. Hebrews often used the title 'adonai', 'my lord', in place of the holy name of God.

Other names for God

According to Exodus 6:3, Abraham and the other patriarchs did not know God by his personal name Yahweh. Instead, they worshipped a God called El Shaddai (Genesis 17:1). But scholars have noted that in the Old Testament the name Yahweh not only appears right from the beginning of the story, but is expressly given to Abraham as the name of the God who led him out of Mesopotamia (Genesis 15:7). In addition, the patriarchs are often said to have worshipped a deity who is called 'the God of the ancestors'.

These differences can be explained by reference to the theory that the first five books of the Old Testament consist of a number of different sources, one of them using the name Yahweh from the very beginning, and another not introducing it until the time of Moses. On this, see the discussion in *The Old Testament Story*, pages 152–56.

But others have suggested that the matter is not quite as straightforward. They draw attention to four features in particular:

● The research of Albrecht Alt has shown that the worship of gods identified as 'the god of my father' (that is 'the god of the ancestors') was widespread among many tribes in the ancient world.

● We also know that the name 'El' was widely used as a name for local gods. In Canaan itself, the Ras Shamra texts depict El as the father of the gods and head of the pantheon at Ugarit.

● Moses apparently knew nothing of the worship of Yahweh until his meeting with Jethro in the desert of Midian. It was certainly in that area that Moses had his experience at the burning bush (Exodus 3:1–6). It is notable that after the exodus from

Egypt Jethro reappears in the story and offers a sacrifice to Yahweh (Exodus 18:10–12).

● When Joshua and his people enter into a solemn agreement to worship only Yahweh, he suggests that both in Mesopotamia and in Egypt their ancestors had worshipped other (pagan) gods (Joshua 24:14–15).

There are two main ways of explaining these apparently diverse facts:

● Some (notably O. Eissfeldt and R. de Vaux) argue that worship of El and worship of Yahweh were originally quite distinct and separate. El was identified by the patriarchs with the high god of Canaan, of whom we know from other sources, and Yahweh was originally the mountain god of the Kenites, whose worship was taken over and reformed by Moses on the basis of the exodus events. Then eventually, either in the days of the judges or in the later monarchy, the worship of Yahweh became dominant and took over its more primitive predecessor.

● Professor F. M. Cross takes a completely different line, arguing that all these names (and others) used for God by the patriarchs referred to the one deity later called Yahweh. To speak of 'the god of the ancestors' was, in his view, just another way of referring to 'El', and 'Yahweh' was the way to address this one God in the context of worship.

Cross's position is certainly closer to the theological stance of the Old Testament itself. As we shall see in a later chapter, the Old Testament was never averse to taking over imagery and ideas from other religious contexts if it could be useful in describing Yahweh and his activities. The patriarchs may well have used traditional ideas from their cultural environment when thinking and speaking about their own experiences of God. But that did not diminish Yahweh's power. It even enhanced it, for it showed that Yahweh was able to do all that the Canaanite El was supposed to do, and much more besides. Whether they knew it or not, it was none other than the God of the exodus – Yahweh himself – who had been the guiding force in their lives from the very beginning.

A hidden God

The Old Testament is dominated by the conviction that God's character is revealed most fully in his dealings with his people, both in history and in personal experience. It is in the common round of everyday life that people meet God. The fact that God is related to the world in which we all live, rather than being relegated to some esoteric, 'heavenly' world, is one of the great strengths of the Old Testament faith. But to many modern people it also seems to be one of its greatest weaknesses. For the plain fact is that we do not normally see events such as the exodus taking place all around us. Nor do many of us have experiences similar to that of Isaiah when he stood in awe before God's glory in the temple. So how realistic and relevant is the Old Testament's picture of God?

Isaiah 6:1–7

It is important for us to observe here that the triumphalist view of God's activity in history and personal experience is by no means the only element in the Old Testament picture of God. To many people in the Old Testament world, God often seemed to be hidden. At the very time when they needed his assistance to make sense of life they found it most difficult to find traces of his activity. The facts of history did not always portray the inevitable progress of an all-powerful God. Nor did the facts of everday life always give Israel the assurance that a living and personal God stood alongside them. There were times when life seemed to be quite the opposite, with evil and suffering as the dominating influences of human existence. How then did God relate to this darker side of life? Was he a God for bad days as well as for good?

The Old Testament writers held a realistic view of life, with all its suffering and darkness as well as light. God carried his people through some bleak years.

The writer of the Book of Job contrasted hope in the natural world – that new growth might come from the stump of a tree – to despair in his personal world. God seemed to have gone for ever.

The Old Testament takes full account of the fact that there are times when it seems that God, far from being powerful and active, is lost in the depths of human pessimism and despair. This honest recognition of God's apparent absence from the scene is most striking in the book of Psalms. Here we have a series of fascinating glimpses into the life of a nation at prayer. Many psalms are great celebrations of joy and optimism, telling the people of God's mighty works and great love for them. These psalms were no doubt used at the great religious festivals, as Israel looked back on the great events of her history and traced God's goodness in them. But for every jubilant psalm there are two or three others in which the worshippers express not joy but sorrow and dismay. Even those with a quiet confidence in God often recognize that he has to be sought in times of 'deepest darkness'. Others complain that life's realities seem inconsistent with the reports of God's mighty deeds in the past.

Psalm 23:4
Psalm 44

The German scholar Hermann Gunkel classified the psalms into five main categories: hymns of praise; individual songs of lament; community laments; individual songs of thanks; and royal psalms. It is significant that only two of these five categories celebrate the triumphs of God in an unreserved way. The other three are all concerned to varying degrees with the fact that God's activity and presence were not always obvious. And when we look closely at the psalms, there are far more of the individual songs of lament than of any other type. Other poems included in this collection express the feelings of the whole nation, as it tried to come to terms with the difference between the great promises that God had made and the less thrilling realities of ordinary life. There is a strong thread of moral and religious realism running through the whole fabric of the Old Testament. God's apparent absence from the world and from human experience is one of its major themes.

● **Personal alienation** This is prominent even in the most striking Old Testament stories. Though Abraham is indeed depic-

Genesis 15:6

ted as a man of great faith who 'put his trust in the Lord', he also finds God's intentions so puzzling and so difficult to reconcile with what he believes about God's character that he is even found arguing

Genesis 18:16–33

with God himself. Moses' experience is quite similar. He had a closer and more direct experience of God than any other Old Testament character, for 'the Lord would speak with Moses face to

Exodus 33:11

face, just as a man speaks with a friend'. But at the same time, Moses' life was full of questions and complaints, as he tried to

Exodus 5:22–23

reconcile God's promises with what he saw going on around him.

Nor are the prophets exempt from feelings of doubt and uncertainty about God's intentions. Take Elijah, for example. He won a great and famous victory in the name of God, as the prophets

1 Kings 18:1–40

of Baal were put to flight and their specious beliefs were repudiated. But almost immediately after that, it seemed as if God had deserted him, and Elijah suffered an extraordinary attack of uncertainty and

1 Kings 19:1–18

doubt about the reality of God's power. And for Jeremiah, doubt and uncertainty were a major influence in his life. On the one hand, God had explicitly told him, 'I chose you before I gave you life, and before

Jeremiah 1:4

you were born I selected you to be a prophet to the nations'. In addition, God had assured him of his continuing love and protection. And yet on the other hand, God seemed singularly reluctant to back him up. A quarter of a century after Jeremiah had first announced the doom of Jerusalem, nothing had happened except that a new mood of national optimism and self-confidence had swept over the city. Jeremiah had to question God's ways: 'Why are wicked men so

Jeremiah 12:1

prosperous? Why do dishonest men succeed?' At another time he even wondered why God allowed him to be born at all: 'Was it only to

Jeremiah 20:18

have trouble and sorrow, to end my life in disgrace?' Of course, the prophet knew that God had indeed spoken to him, but that did not make it any easier to come to terms with God's apparent remoteness. The passages in which Jeremiah addresses his complaints to God (the 'Confessions') are remarkable for their frankness, and show the

Jeremiah 11:18–23; 12:1–6;
15:10–21; 17:14–18; 18:18–23;
20:7–18

depths of despair and questioning to which even those with a personal knowledge of God in their lives can be driven.

Wrestling with a hidden God

The apparent hiddenness of God is a major theme of one of the great masterpieces of the Old Testament: the book of Job. The book itself begins with an idyllic description of the life of its hero. He was a successful man in every respect, surrounded not only by the material trappings of prosperity but also by an affectionate family group. He was also exceedingly upright and religious.

His lifestyle and disposition both show him as a paradigm of virtue. But then things change. God, depicted here as the president of a heavenly court, receives a formal request from the prosecutor (Satan) who suggests that Job is righteous only because he finds that it pays handsome dividends. And so the prosecutor is given permission to put him to the test to ascertain the value of his faith. One calamity after another comes upon Job and his family, until he is reduced to misery and poverty – the exact opposite of what he was at the beginning (Job 1:1–2:10).

At this point, the ancient story is left behind. The author of Job was not just a storyteller. From a literary standpoint, his book belongs to the 'wisdom' literature of the Old Testament, and his main concern was to answer the questions that were raised by the story. It was a simple and well-known problem: If God rules the world, why do good people suffer so much? Wise men from Babylon to Egypt and beyond had wrestled with this problem long

before the author of Job. But two things gave it special urgency in Israel: Israel believed that God was active in controlling the life of this world; and Israel also believed that God acted in accordance with strict concepts of morality.

The standard answer to the problem was easy, and is in fact represented in some other wisdom books, notably Proverbs: those who were prosperous must be good, and those who suffered must be evil. But it is often difficult to reconcile that with the facts, especially in the case of a person like Job. Of course, his friends could not see that. For although they sympathized with Job

The Jews exiled in Babylon longed to return home. But during this time of heartache they learned new truths about God's relationship with them wherever they were.

in his suffering they were quite sure that, whatever he thought, he must have sinned against God and brought his suffering on himself. Job knew he had not done so, and he was convinced that the easy theology of his friends was quite misguided. Not that this made it any easier for him to see God at work in his own life: 'I have searched in the east, but God is not there; I have not found him when I searched in the west.' But he never abandoned his certainty that, though God may be hidden for a time, he is still there: 'God has been at work in the north and the south', and it is just that 'I have not seen him' (23:8–9). Indeed, it was worse than just

being blind to God's purpose, for it was God's very hiddenness that concerned Job most of all: 'It is God, not the dark, that makes me afraid ...'(23:17).

The meaningless circle of Job's existence is eventually broken when, after more conventional wisdom from his friends, God himself confronts the sufferer in a great storm (38:1–41:34). God reminds Job of his own greatness and might by drawing his attention to the complexity of the world and its workings. In the face of this, Job can place his own questions in their proper perspective: 'I know, Lord, that you are all-powerful; that you can do everything you want' (42:1).

But what is the answer to the question? Certainly there is no intellectual discussion here of the presence and power of evil in the world. But it is typical of the Old Testament that even a topic such as this should not be dealt with in an abstract, philosophical way. God is known to men and women not in flights of fancy but in the reality of divine encounter. Job had appealed to God to answer him – and he did. Not in a way that he might have expected, but in a way that ultimately reminded him that, however difficult it might be to understand life's bitterest experiences, and however hard it might be to perceive God at work, nevertheless he was there. And to those who were prepared to seek him out – unlike the friends who looked for easy answers – God would ultimately reveal himself.

Another Old Testament book which tackles similar questions is Ecclesiastes. But its answer is very different. Indeed, it lays so much emphasis on God's apparent absence from the world that the Jewish rabbis were reluctant to accept it as a part of scripture. Like Job, this book has no mention of the great events of Israel's history in which God's hand had so clearly been seen. But unlike Job, it has no clear conviction that God's workings can be seen

anywhere in the world at all. Job never actually loses sight of God, even if only in the negative sense that he blames God for his misfortune. But for Ecclesiastes, life is essentially meaningless in itself. That is not to say that life need be miserable and uninteresting. Ecclesiastes does not actually deny that God exists, for all life's goods come from him (2:24–26; 3:13; 8:15). But the whole book is shot through with a kind of practical atheism. Whether or not God exists is really irrelevant, for the author does not see much evidence of his involvement in the practical issues of everyday living. The most anyone can do is to try to enjoy what they have while they are here to enjoy it.

This might seem a very negative attitude to take towards God. But it is more faithful to human experience than the fanciful and unsatisfying theology of Job's friends. The fact is that human life cannot be reduced to simple formulas. Nor can faith in God. Not only Ecclesiastes but the whole of the Old Testament bears witness to the fact that a faith which comes too easily has a certain lack of reality. The experience of honest and searching doubt is often the prelude to a deeper and more satisfying understanding of God and his ways and not to a loss of faith.

● **National despair** It was not only individuals who often had to look hard to find God at work in their lives. The whole Jewish nation found itself in a similar crisis after the fall of Jerusalem to the Babylonian king Nebuchadnezzar in 586 BC. A once-proud nation had been brought to its knees by events that shattered all their expectations of God. Looking to the past, they could recall God's gracious actions through the great heroes of their nation. They could remind themselves of God's unfailing promises to previous generations. But what value could be placed on such a glorious past in the light of the harsh realities of exile in a strange land? The promises had apparently failed, and evidence of God's involvement with his people was hard to find.

Much of the Old Testament story was hammered into shape on the anvil of this experience. Its pages often reflect the deeply felt anguish of those who survived this great tragedy, as they asked the inevitable question: Why should this have happened in a world controlled by God? In response to that the Deuteronomistic History asserted quite plainly that national disgrace was the outcome of national sin. But in looking to the past it did not give a simplistic explanation of the present. For although it emphasized God's great goodness to his people in events such as the exodus, or the establishment of David's throne in Jerusalem, it also reminded them that there had been many a crisis in the past too. The exodus itself had been God's answer to a grave crisis faced by the enslaved tribes in Egypt. God can hardly have seemed very real to them in Egypt – but one of the lessons of history was that God's mighty power had often burst in to change the lives of those who were least expecting it.

There could be no doubt that the exiles were suffering as a result of their nation's disobedience. A God whose character was defined in terms of justice and moral standards could not easily turn a blind eye to the rotten state of Jewish society. But though it might seem as if the stringency of God's justice was greater than the power of his love, nevertheless he would still be faithful to his promises and in the end would bring blessing to his people.

This was the view that finally triumphed and transformed the dead husks of exile into the seed corn of new life. Just as in the experience of the prophets and of people such as Job, so here there is no real effort to explain why God seemed to be hidden from his people. But there is a clear practical message for those who found it difficult to see God at work in their lives. As men and women contemplated the suffering and injustice of their present existence, they were forced to confess that God really is inscrutable in his ways. Yet alongside this they could place the evidence of his mighty acts in history and in personal experience, both of which gave the assurance that though God may be hidden by the gloom of present experience, he was still active in his world. To those who trusted him the future would present something even more glorious than what had been lost.

At Mount Sinai, in the wilderness between Egypt and Canaan, God made himself known to his people as the giver of the law. It was an encounter that permanently changed their understanding of themselves and of God.

How is God known?

Finally, we must turn briefly to consider some of the assumptions behind the Old Testament's view of God and his relationship to his people. Two themes are especially important here.

God's grace

It was not unusual in the ancient world for the gods to be portrayed almost as if they were a race of superhumans. In one way it is almost inevitable that when people talk about God they should use human analogies to do so. The Old Testament is no exception. It describes God in very bold figures of speech, asserting that he has hands and eyes, and that he cries or laughs, and has emotions comparable to human feelings. But for all that, there is a clear consciousness that in his essential being God is quite different from people. His actions are not therefore rationalizations of the way men and women behave. Nor is he to be bullied and cajoled by magic, as if he could easily be blackmailed. If God makes himself known in the lives of men and women, it is because he has taken the initiative.

This affirmation is central to the Old Testament faith: all relationships with God are based on God's own actions in grace and love. God wishes to commit himself to the whole human race, and as a means to that end he calls Abraham. In doing so, he acts freely, and his only motive is to share his love with the people who live in his world. At every significant point of the story thereafter, the Old Testament emphasizes that God's own gracious actions are the starting-point for a meaningful relationship with him. The exodus itself happens because God sees their plight and takes pity on them, not because the enslaved tribes ask for it. And individual men and women can enjoy fellowship with him simply because of God's love for them and not because of any inherent claim they might have on God. No one can work up a sense of God's presence for themselves. He is not found by personal introspection: God bursts into a person's life from outside. He is, to use theological jargon, transcendent. The Old Testament uses more picturesque language to describe the same thing: 'The Lord is great and is to be highly praised; his greatness is beyond understanding.'

Genesis 12:1–3

Psalm 145:3

God's word

How then does God communicate? A simple answer would be: through his mighty acts. There is much truth in this, and the Old Testament often claims that God has revealed himself to his people through his great actions in history and personal experience. Indeed, much of the Old Testament's moral law is based on the assumption that the way God acts displays the kind of God he is. But a moment's thought will show that this answer is not entirely satisfactory.

Take the exodus, which for Israel was the greatest revelation of God's character and will. For the escaping slaves, and later generations who shared their perspective, this was the crucial event in which God was made known. But what did it mean to the Egyptians? We do not know, of course, for Egyptian annals nowhere mention such an event. But it is quite certain that the exodus was not for them a means of divine encounter in which the God Yahweh met them and changed their national history. Something else was needed to transform the bare happenings of history into a message from God.

This is always the way, of course. The 'bare facts' of history only gain significance when they are placed in an appropriate context. A modern historian does not simply record isolated incidents from the past: he tries to explain them in relation to other incidents, in order to make sense out of what has taken place. The Old Testament does the same, and what makes its story so distinctive is the interpretation that is given to the events which it describes. As historians and prophets looked back to the nation's past they saw God himself at work. They did not view the past as just a historical chain of cause and effect.

If that was the end of the story, we might conclude that the Old Testament faith was little more than a historian's theory – a neat way of giving coherence and meaning to a rather amorphous collection of events that had happened at different times and places over many generations. But there is more to it than that. For the prophets did not interpret the history of their people in retrospect. They claimed to announce it before it took place. When Amos issued his scathing denunciations of Samarian society, and declared that it would soon come to an end, there was no sign of such an end. Indeed, the nation was enjoying a period of prosperity unparalleled at any other time in its history. When Jeremiah announced the doom of Jerusalem, the mood of self-satisfaction that was sweeping the city led people to regard him as a madman. But they – and the other prophets – persisted with their message because they were convinced that what they were saying was the word of God to their people. The earlier story of the exodus was no different. For Moses himself is portrayed as a prophet – indeed, the greatest of all prophets – announcing the exodus while the people were yet in slavery!

Deuteronomy 34:10–12

It is difficult for us today to grasp this, and still more difficult to understand it. But it is an essential part of the Old Testament's picture of God. The Old Testament never claims to be able to fathom all the depths of God's personality, and there are many aspects of his work that can never be fully understood. But this one conviction runs throughout all its writings: the living God is not a static being, remote and irrelevant to the lives of ordinary people. He is a God who acts, and a God who speaks in order that men and women might have a full and meaningful relationship with him and with one another.

The prophets

We have mentioned individuals called prophets in connexion with our discussion here of the way God communicated with his people. So who were these prophets – and how did they relate to the national religious life of Old Testament times?

All the greatest prophets are, of course, known to us through various Old Testament books which bear their names. In *The Old Testament Story* we have given extensive consideration to the careers of these people and the messages they delivered. At one time it was fashionable to suppose that it was through the activity of such messengers that a primitive and superstitious popular religiosity was transformed into the high ideals of morality that we find in the Old Testament today. The great preaching prophets from Amos to Ezekiel undoubtedly had a profound and far-reaching effect on the life of

their nation. But Old Testament prophecy as a whole is much more complex than that simplistic explanation suggests.

We are alerted to this complexity as soon as we appreciate that the Old Testament uses four different Hebrew expressions for 'prophet'. Some passages seem to suggest that the terminology changed with the passage of time (1 Samuel 9:11), but in reality we cannot now tell the technical difference between these terms. The fact that the terminology is so diverse, however, clearly suggests that prophets differed from each other, and that prophecy was not just a single social and religious phenomenon. Indeed, we find people called prophets operating in many different social contexts: as diviners (1 Samuel 9:1–25); as ecstatics, often in groups who are distinguished by special marks and clothing (1 Samuel 10:5–8;

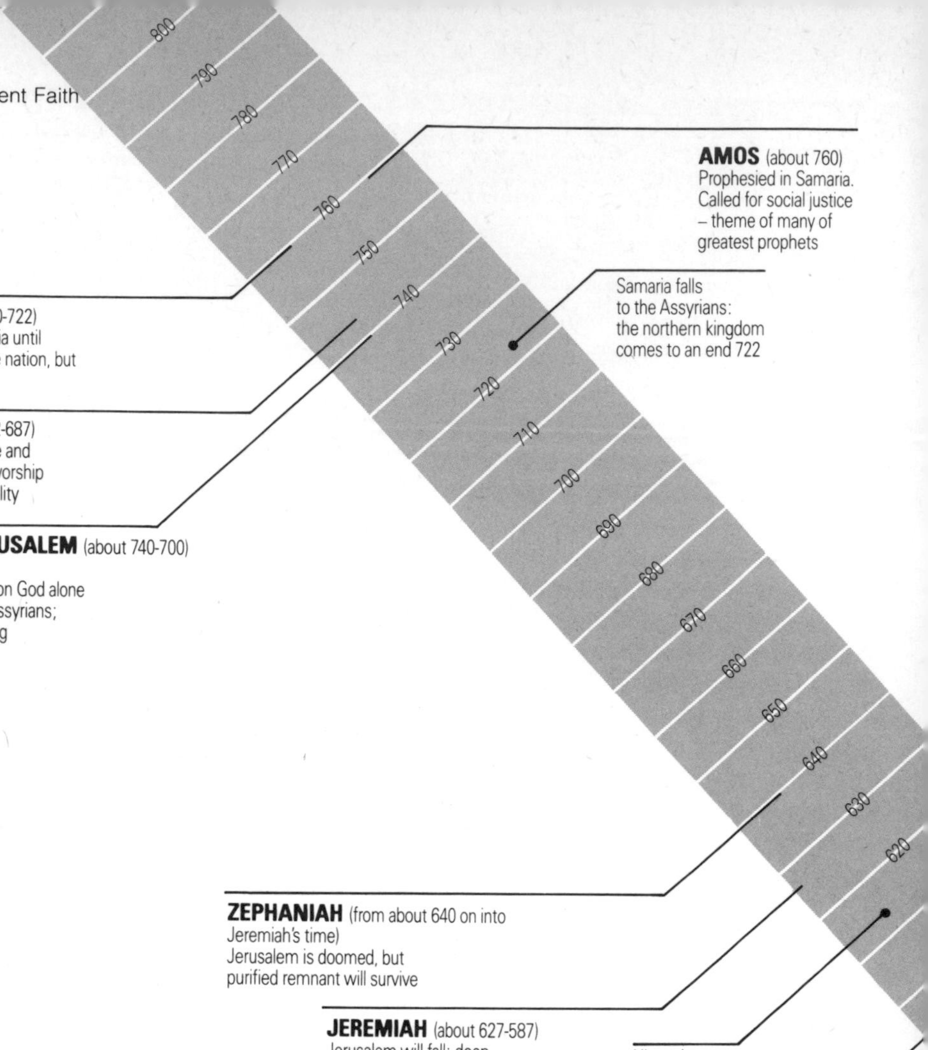

800
790
780
770
760
750
740
730
720
710
700
690
680
670
660
650
640
630
620

AMOS (about 760)
Prophesied in Samaria.
Called for social justice
– theme of many of
greatest prophets

Samaria falls
to the Assyrians:
the northern kingdom
comes to an end 722

HOSEA (about 760-722)
Prophesied in Samaria until
its fall. God will judge nation, but
also loves it deeply

MICAH (about 742-687)
Concerned for justice and
true religion; hated worship
separated from morality

ISAIAH OF JERUSALEM (about 740-700)
Great vision of God;
nation must depend on God alone
for protection from Assyrians;
predicts a coming king

ZEPHANIAH (from about 640 on into
Jeremiah's time)
Jerusalem is doomed, but
purified remnant will survive

JEREMIAH (about 627-587)
Jerusalem will fall; deep
concern for faith and repentance;
prophet's inward grief;
promise of new covenant

Nineveh,
Assyria's capital,
falls 612

EZEKIEL (about 593-570)
Prophesied in Babylon;
Jerusalem will finally fall;
promise of future return and revival

DANIEL
Story of Jew in exile who
refused to compromise faith;
visions of the future

ISAIAH OF BABYLON
(probably during the exile and after)
God will save, restore
and revive his people;
poems of suffering servant

JOEL? (time of writing unknown)
Plague of locusts used as
basis for call to repentance

JONAH? (time of writing unknown)
Story of prophet sent
to call Nineveh to repent

OBADIAH (after 586)
Against Edomites for adding to
Jerusalem's misfortunes

LAMENTATIONS (after 586)
Five poems lamenting the
destruction of Jerusalem

The Prophets:
their time and their message

There were prophets in Israel from early days, including Moses as well as Elijah and Elisha. From the eighth century BC to the fifth, the prophecies of the foremost prophets were collected into books which have survived.

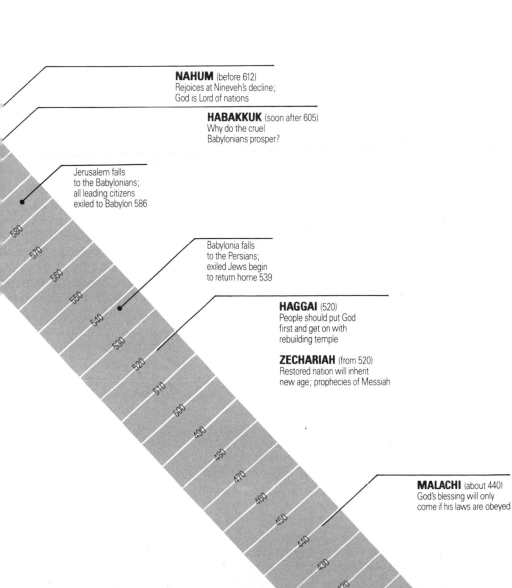

NAHUM (before 612)
Rejoices at Nineveh's decline;
God is Lord of nations

HABAKKUK (soon after 605)
Why do the cruel
Babylonians prosper?

Jerusalem falls
to the Babylonians;
all leading citizens
exiled to Babylon 586

Babylonia falls
to the Persians;
exiled Jews begin
to return home 539

HAGGAI (520)
People should put God
first and get on with
rebuilding temple

ZECHARIAH (from 520)
Restored nation will inherit
new age; prophecies of Messiah

MALACHI (about 440)
God's blessing will only
come if his laws are obeyed

580 570 560 550 540 530 520 510 500 490 480 470 460 450 440 430 420 410

19:18–24; 1 Kings 20:35–43; 2 Kings 1:8; 2:23–24; 4:38; 6:12); as royal court prophets (1 Samuel 22:5; 2 Samuel 12:1–15; 24:11; 1 Kings 20:35–43); as war prophets (Judges 4:4–9; 1 Kings 20; 22:1–28); as cultic prophets (1 Samuel 10:5–8; 2 Kings 4:18–25); as 'false' prophets (1 Kings 22; Micah 3:5–6; Isaiah 9:15; Ezekiel 13:2; Jeremiah 6:14). And there may well be more circumstances in which prophets played an important part in the life of the community.

Culturally (and therefore religiously), prophecy was a very diverse phenomenon. Some prophets seem to have operated in more than one way. For instance, Samuel is at one time a seer, when he tells Saul about his lost asses (1 Samuel 9:11), but he then goes on to give specific messages about the kingship in a more spontaneous kind of prophetic utterance (1 Samuel 10:1–8). Yet others, for example Amos, claim not to have been real 'professional' prophets at all! (Amos 7:12–15).

A number of models have been used by scholars to try to explain the form and function of Old Testament prophecy. Here we shall notice just four of the more significant approaches:

A history of religions approach

In view of our ever-increasing knowledge of social and religious situations throughout the ancient world, it is natural to try to compare Old Testament prophets with similar characters elsewhere. One of the earliest exponents of this view was the Scandinavian scholar Alfred Haldar. According to him, prophecy was a phenomenon found in the context of organized religion (the cult). A close analysis of texts from Babylon (Old Babylon, 1894–1595 BC) discerned two elements in it:

Mahhu priests/prophets, who specialized in wild, ecstatic trance-induced behaviour.

Baru priests/prophets, who specialized in divination. That is, they would be asked a specific question, the answer to which they would discover by throwing dice, or by astrological speculations, or by offering sacrifices and examining the entrails of the dead animals in order to discover the will of the gods.

Haldar claimed to find Old Testament evidence for this pattern, mainly in the dual functions of Samuel. He believed other isolated passages provide evidence for the work of 'divination corporations' (Isaiah 21:6–10)

or sacrificial inspection (Psalm 5:3). But this view of the nature of prophecy is difficult to substantiate from the Old Testament:

● Although the Old Testament does have evidence for wild behaviour on occasion (1 Samuel 10:9–13), and of giving specific answers to questions (1 Samuel 9:3–20), it is not the most obvious form of Old Testament prophecy. There is a good deal more evidence for a more 'rational' kind of prophecy. Indeed, when Jeremiah finds a message in a potter's workshop (Jeremiah 18), or in a basket of figs (Jeremiah 24), it is at least arguable that his message is essentially the result of rational deliberation on the everyday happenings of life, and has nothing at all to do with special emotional or religious experiences.

● Even when prophets do answer specific questions ('divination'), the Old Testament provides no evidence that they manipulated special objects such as dice or sacrifices in order to arrive at an answer (1 Samuel 9:17ff; 1 Kings 22).

● To use such technical means of divination required special training and a lot of practice. Again, there is no Old Testament evidence of the prophets being trained at all, and a fair amount to the contrary (for example, Amos 7:12–15).

Others have looked to Egypt and Syria as sources of possible models for Old Testament prophecy. Mari is another society in which there was evidently a kind of 'prophecy'. Texts from there speak of 'prophets' who were religious functionaries, of trance prophets, and of yet others who brought messages to the attention of the king (bureaucrats of a sort). At one time or another, all this material has been regarded as a possible 'source' of Old Testament prophecy, and there is no doubt that much of it can help us to a better understanding of the Old Testament. But there is unlikely to be any direct line of connexion between them:

● Recent study has shown that the social functions performed by diviners, ecstatics, and so on can arise in any society, ancient or modern, quite independently of external direct contact.

● There is in the Old Testament a much wider diversity than in any of the comparative materials so far examined. There is far less emphasis on divination here than elsewhere – indeed, Samuel is the odd man out as far as the Old Testament is concerned.

● In general, the concerns of Old

Testament prophecy are the great sweep of history and the meaning of human life on a broad scale, not the trivialities of everyday life.

A psychological approach

Julius Wellhausen (1844–1918) argued that the prophets were essentially inspired individuals, who changed the form of Old Testament religious belief. The presence of apparently irrational prophetic behaviour in certain Old Testament stories seemed to suggest that a useful perspective on the prophets would be gained by asking what it was that made them such exceptional people. This line of enquiry was especially associated with the work of Hermann Gunkel (1862–1932), who concluded that the key to understanding the prophets was 'ecstasy'. By this he meant the kind of irrational, over-emotional behaviour that is familiar from many contexts the

Some of the Old Testament prophets used powerful symbols to convey God's word, as when Jeremiah watched a potter making a new pot from the spoiled remains of clay that had not formed as he intended.

world over. Modern examples could be found in extreme forms of Pentecostalism, such as snake handlers or Holy Rollers, though this sort of wild behaviour is by no means peculiar to the Judeo-Christian religious tradition.

Gunkel described the prophetic experience in the following way: 'When such an ecstasy seizes him, the prophet ... loses command of his limbs; he staggers and stutters like a drunken man; his ordinary sense of what is decent deserts him; he feels an impulse to do all kinds of strange actions ... strange ideas and emotions come over him ... he is seized by that sensation of hovering which we know from our own dreams...'

We all know of such cases of abnormal behaviour today; and we must recognize that such mass hypnotism is not difficult to produce, given the right people and the right circumstances. But is this what Old Testament prophecy is all about? To answer that question, scholars such as Gunkel looked to Canaanite prophecy (of which they knew next to nothing apart from 1 Kings 18!). Such evidence as they had for this certainly showed the prophets of Baal producing ecstatic hysteria by a series of self-inflicted moves – music, shouting, dancing, drink, drugs, and so on. And when we look at the Old Testament it is certainly possible to find such things in Israel. The best example would be the prophets whom Saul met (1 Samuel 10), though there are others (2 Kings 2; 1 Kings 22).

The real problem with this approach is that it explains only a small fragment of the total Old Testament evidence. Even Gunkel himself had to admit that, if the earliest prophets just raved in ecstasy as an end in itself, that certainly was not what the great prophets did. He reached the conclusion that prophecy must have developed from ecstatic mass hysteria into a more rational phenomenon. But others have assessed the evidence differently:

● Some identify the ecstatics with 'false prophets', by contrast to the 'real' prophets who were rational speakers. But there are many indications that the great prophets could also have unusual emotional experiences (Jeremiah 4:19; 23:9; Ezekiel 1:1–3:15).

● Recognizing this, it is possible to try to distinguish the experiences of the great prophets from the content of their messages. Perhaps the messages were delivered in a rational way after the experiences, but with no particular reference to what had gone before.

The fact is, however, that none of these explanations is wholly satisfying. The Old Testament itself makes none of these distinctions, and all the prophets mentioned there have unusual experiences of one sort or another. The way in which the experiences are related to life situations seems to depend on the circumstances of the moment. Although analysis of ecstasy and other related emotional states can shed some light on prophetic experience, it is clear that a full understanding of the prophets is not to be found there.

A literary approach

It was the search for a meaningful life situation that led Claus Westermann to

One great act of God was in bringing the Jews back to Jerusalem from exile in Babylon. The return was announced by the prophets Isaiah and Ezekiel. It heralded a fresh start for their national faith.

begin to analyze the literary form of the prophetic messages in the Old Testament. In the ancient world, the way a person spoke was determined by their context to a much greater extent than it is today. By analyzing the forms of prophetic speech we can therefore set it in various contexts, such as the law court (Amos 7:16–17; Micah 2:1–4), the wisdom school (Jeremiah 17:5–8), the worship context (Habakkuk; Isaiah 40–55), or the royal court ('Thus says ...', a royal messenger speech-form). That being the case, it can be argued that the prophets must have been essentially ordinary people, whose background lay in the official functions of these different life situations. It has even been suggested that the descriptions of 'visions' and other 'ecstatic' experiences could perhaps be stylistic devices, rather than literal descriptions of things that happened.

This way of looking at the prophets and their messages has added enormously to our understanding of them. But by itself, it can lead to a one-sided view of their functions:

● It is to some extent a reaction against the extreme 'ecstatic' view: instead of the prophet being seen as an innovator, he is here viewed as a conventional person operating within the normal structures of society. But the fact is that the element of 'ecstasy' is still there in the Old Testament, and cannot be disposed of quite so simply.

● Then there is the question of a jump from literary form to life situation. A person who uses a legal form is not necessarily a lawyer. He may be just a good communicator, using language that he knows will be especially evocative and challenging to his hearers.

A theological/cultic approach

A century ago, Julius Wellhausen was arguing that the prophets had broken completely with cultic worship in ancient Israel, and were attempting to introduce morality into what had hitherto been a barren and empty form of ritualism. Today, many scholars would argue the exact opposite, suggesting that the religious life of Israel had started with a covenant based on a distinctly moral view of God, and that the prophets were closely associated with this covenant ideal and with its celebration in the context of worship.

There can be no doubt that the idea of a 'covenant' is at the heart of the Old Testament faith. The whole collection of Old Testament books centres on the unmistakable conviction that God had burst into the lives of his people because of his own unmerited love ('grace'), and that as a result of this his people were called upon to respond by a loving obedience in return. When we talk of 'the covenant', this is all that we mean: the responsive obedience of the people, consequent upon their experience of God's grace. In historical terms, that experience had been demonstrated most dramatically in the events of the exodus and what followed, and this is a major theme in the messages of many of the greatest prophets. It was also celebrated regularly in the great worship festivals that marked the progress of Israel's religious life.

Scholars such as Sigmund Mowinckel have no doubt exaggerated the role of the prophets in this religious worship. But it certainly makes sense to see them as guardians of the covenant faith. It explains why they spoke in full expectation that people would listen. For they were calling them back to their spiritual roots.

It is fruitless to try to restrict our understanding of the Old Testament prophets to just one category or another. The whole phenomenon of prophecy in the Old Testament is so diverse that perhaps we need to speak individually of particular prophets rather than trying to speak of them all in one breath. But they were all conscious of speaking in the name of God himself, and applying the standards of the covenant faith to the ongoing life of nations and individuals.

3 God and the world

Discovering God in nature and history

IN THE last chapter, we saw that God's most characteristic method of communication in the Old Testament was through the events of history: the exodus from Egypt; the establishment of David's royal city in Jerusalem; even the exile. When correctly understood and explained, all these things told the people of Old Testament times what God was really like.

We would be quite wrong though to think that the Old Testament faith is concerned exclusively with the events of Israel's history. The heart of the Old Testament is certainly to be found in the stories that begin with Israel's ancestor Abraham and end with Judah's exile in Babylon. But there is a lot more than this in its pages. The early

Genesis 1 — 11

stories of the book of Genesis, most of the psalms, and all the 'wisdom' books (Proverbs, Ecclesiastes, Job, Song of Solomon) are only loosely related to the great themes of Israel's salvation history. In their own way, they all deal with the universal experience of men and women everywhere as they try to come to grips with the world in which they live. Moreover, these particular parts of the Old Testament have many close connexions with the religious literature of other nations of the time. Their central concern is not with the unique and unrepeatable experience of Israel. Instead, they place God's activities in an international perspective, and suggest that his claims over people's lives are universal because his handiwork is evident in the very stuff of which the world is made.

Some scholars have suggested that the Old Testament faith developed an interest in God's relationship to the world at quite a late date. It is certainly true that during the years of the Babylonian exile (which began in 597 BC), many aspects of the Old Testament faith were worked out in their final detail. The majestic poetry of the

Isaiah 40 — 55

second part of the book of Isaiah certainly reflects that period. One of its most striking features is the imagery in which it celebrates God's power over the world of nature. Some of this language, and

Genesis 1:1 — 2:4

that found in the creation story of the book of Genesis, seems to have connexions with Mesopotamian stories of how the world was made. On that basis, it is suggested that the Old Testament faith was expanded at this period, moving the emphasis away from God's acts in history at a time when he seemed to be doing very little for his people.

This is a widely-held view, repeated by many Old Testament scholars. But it is far too simplistic. Some of the Old Testament's most sophisticated thinking about God and creation may well have been articulated during the exile. But a number of factors suggest that God's relationship to the natural world must have been an important part of Israel's life long before that:

● Most of the psalms reflect the worship and liturgy of pre-exilic Israel. They show quite clearly that Yahweh was worshipped as the Creator of the world long before Israel had any firsthand dealings with Babylon. There is no creation story as such in the psalms, but creation imagery (often drawn from the religious traditions of other nations) is used so often that belief in God as Creator was obviously a fundamental theme of worship in the temple at Jerusalem.

● We also know that the gods' role in relation to the natural world was fundamental to most other religions of the time. The texts from Ugarit have not so far disclosed a fully developed Canaanite creation story comparable with those found in ancient Babylon, but all the activities of the Canaanite gods and goddesses were related to the workings of the natural world. One of the first questions the invading tribes had to answer was whether Baal or Yahweh was in control of their world. It is inconceivable that they should have waited for half a millenium before giving an answer. As the Old Testament story unfolds, one of its major concerns is how Yahweh, the God of the exodus, related to the demands of settled agricultural life. The prevailing popular view was that the world of nature and the world of the gods were one and the same. So the actions of gods such as the Canaanite Baal would explain the mysterious workings of the world of nature in which Palestinian farmers had to eke out a precarious living. Was Yahweh only a God of history – and did that mean the natural world was controlled by worship of deities such as Baal and Anat? The story of Elijah shows that this was a pressing issue as early as the ninth century BC. A hundred years later the prophet Amos denounced the behaviour of non-Israelite people in a way that would

1 Kings 17:1 — 19:18

The Israelites began to discover the character of God in their time as nomads in the wilderness. But the discovery continued as they settled in the fertile land of Canaan and began to live an agricultural life.

Amos 1:3 — 2:3

only have made sense on the basis of a coherent set of beliefs about God and the world which he had made.

● Similar questions must also have presented themselves on a personal level. After all, only one relatively small group of people had witnessed the amazing events of the exodus and the conquest of the land. Not many had any direct contact with the great promises made to David. And, mercifully, few had been left in Jerusalem to witness its final humiliation at the hands of Nebuchadnezzar. If these were the key events in which God revealed himself to his people, then how could the rest of them hear his voice? Though the great events of the past could be celebrated in regular religious festivals, the fact was that the everyday experience of ordinary people was more closely tied to the world of nature than to the world of great and unrepeatable historical events. And that in itself must have required the development of some coherent belief about Israel's God and his relationship to the natural world.

Genesis 12:1–3

● From as far back as the call of Abraham, the Old Testament suggests that God's intervention in Israel's history was to be a means to the salvation of all nations. This insight was clearly central to the Old Testament faith, and is underlined by all the great prophets. It was often misunderstood, of course. The easy-going national optimism that often dominated popular thinking in both Israel and Judah could easily lead people to conclude that other nations were of no concern to God. But to overcome such misunderstanding, it must have been necessary to know precisely how Israel was related to other nations. The stories of creation are the only parts of the Old Testament which answer that question.

Genesis 2:4–25

● At least significant parts of the Genesis stories were certainly composed long before the exile in Babylon, for their imagery, and the assumptions made about the countryside and the moods of the weather, clearly point to a Palestinian background.

Psalm 24:1

In the light of all these considerations, we must conclude that belief in God as the Creator was a significant and integral part of the Old Testament faith from relatively early times. Like other aspects of that faith, it developed and matured as time passed. But one of its basic convictions was that 'The world and all that is in it belong to the Lord ...' Its importance is stressed by the fact that we meet this subject on the opening page of Genesis. For here, and in what follows, Israel's ancient thinkers have preserved for us some of the most fundamental aspects of their faith.

Thinking about the world

Genesis 1 — 11

The first section of the book of Genesis is one of the most important parts of the whole Old Testament. In the stories of creation, the fall, Cain and Abel, the flood and the tower of Babel, we have a concise summary of the whole of the Old Testament faith. Such basic themes as the character of God, the nature of the world, and the meaning of human existence are presented here with an imaginative subtlety that has given these chapters a place among the great classics of world literature. Yet we need be neither theologians nor literary critics to grasp their message. Like the parables of Jesus, these stories have a universal appeal to people in all times and places, for they speak to the deepest needs of men and women, and give an honest answer to questions that have perplexed the world's greatest thinkers.

Understanding the Genesis stories

This makes it all the more surprising that the early chapters of Genesis should ever have become a subject of controversy. Yet it can hardly be denied that in the last 200 years they have been the subject of so many complex debates that ordinary Bible readers are often at a loss to know what to do with them. Huge volumes have been written in answer to this question, and anything we can say here must inevitably be brief and incomplete. But two things seem to be of central importance here:

● Ever since Charles Darwin published his *Origin of Species* in 1859, the Genesis creation story has been used by the protagonists in many debates about science and religion. Scientists imbued with a materialistic world-view have sometimes claimed that these chapters demonstrate the naivety of religious belief – and fervent believers have just as often replied that the creation stories prove the inadequacy of modern scientific endeavour. In some Christian

Many ancient peoples have their myths, as is shown in these mysterious carvings on Easter Island. But how well does the category of 'myth' fit the stories at the beginning of Genesis?

circles, it is taken for granted that Christian doctrine requires these chapters to be taken as a scientific account of the origins of the universe. This position inevitably sets the Old Testament at variance with the findings of science, and identifies a biblical faith with what most people would regard as an outmoded view of how the world works.

We need to remember that all this is a fairly recent development. Earlier generations of Bible scholars were much less inclined to try to force the book of Genesis into the strait-jacket of a scientific textbook. The great sixteenth-century scholar, John Calvin, was asked by the literalists of his day how he could make sense of the statement that the dome of the sky ('firmament') was separating 'the water under it from the water above it'. Even to the scientists of his day, it seemed unlikely that there could be waters above the sky. In his *Commentary on Genesis*, Calvin agreed with them, describing such a notion as 'opposed to common sense, and quite incredible'. He found those who regarded Genesis as a book of science equally incredible, and went on to assert that 'to my mind, this is a certain principle, that nothing is here treated of but the visible form of the world. He who would learn astronomy, and other recondite arts, let him go elsewhere ...' Calvin was quite clear that the Old Testament was never intended to be a book of science, and that reading it as if it was would only confuse and distort its essential message. The Old Testament writers, he argued, simply took for granted the sort of world-view that was widely held in their day. This assumed that the world was like a flat disc, set upon pillars below, and with the sky arching over it like a dome. The Old Testament writers never discuss whether this was scientifically correct or not: it was not necessary for them to do so, for this was not why they were writing. Calvin describes details such as this as only props on the main stage – background detail to reinforce the fact that the Old Testament's message was relevant to the world in which ordinary people lived.

● The message, here as elsewhere in the Old Testament, is about God. We have already seen this when we considered the meaning of the great events of Israel's history. The story of the exodus, for instance, was recorded not just because it happened, but because it demonstrated God's active and loving concern for his people. A casual reader can see that even in the Old Testament's history

Genesis 1:6–7

The great ziggurat at Ur on the Euphrates was built in about 2100 BC. It has recently been partially reconstructed. Such a structure may lie behind the story of the tower of Babel.

books, the main emphasis is on theological explanation, not on historical analysis. The great Deuteronomistic History which forms the core of the Old Testament story certainly explains and applies the lessons that are to be drawn from what it records. So do the books of the Chronicler. And Genesis itself was no doubt compiled and issued in its present form as a tangible answer to the problem faced by a generation far removed from the events which it describes.

Deuteronomy — 2 Kings

Nor does the Old Testament always use historical events to convey its essential message. The hymns and prayers of the psalms, the sermons of the prophets and the writings of Israel's wise men, all explain important aspects of God's dealings with his people. As the prophets loved to point out, the message ('the word of the Lord') was the really important thing, not the medium through which it was communicated. Of course, those who do not share the prophets' faith could read the Old Testament histories and see nothing more than a diffuse account of a small and second-rate Middle Eastern power. We can do the same with the creation stories, and see nothing but an apparently factual account of the doings of two people in a garden full of plants and animals. At a more sophisticated level, we can join those modern scholars who think of these stories as a collection of folk tales designed to answer such everyday questions as why snakes have no legs, why weeds grow in fields, or why in ancient Israel it was better to be a shepherd than a farmer. But if these are the only things we see as we read the book of Genesis, then we have missed the most crucial points that its author was intending to make. For he was not concerned with the needs of ancient farmers, nor even with some kind of primitive sociology, but with God himself. Just as Jesus often explained important aspects of his message by using the familiar experiences of everyday life, so the editor of Genesis starts from the common experiences of human life, and goes on to show how God can relate to both the joys and the miseries of the world and its people.

The stories as literature

The Old Testament is a library of many different kinds of literature. In its pages we find not only history, but law, drama, poetry, sermons, political tracts, and much more. They are all held together by their common conviction that God is at the centre of all human life and activity. But before we can fully understand the significance of any particular passage, we must obviously decide what sort of literature we are dealing with. We would not read a political tract in the same way as we might read legal documents. The kind of analytical judgment required to understand history would be quite out of place in the more aesthetic world of poetry and drama. So how can we classify these early stories in Genesis?

● **Myth?** Many books on the Old Testament refer to them as 'myths'. But this is not a particularly helpful term to use. Most people think of a myth as something that is untrue. Scholars do not normally use it in this sense, but even they have no agreed definition of it. It is commonly used to mean at least three different things:

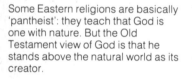

Some Eastern religions are basically 'pantheist': they teach that God is one with nature. But the Old Testament view of God is that he stands above the natural world as its creator.

1. A myth can be simply a story about gods and goddesses and their doings, described as if they were human beings. There are many examples of this in Greek and Hindu mythology.

2. Myth can also be a technical term for what takes place during a religious rite. In ancient Babylon, for instance, the annual New Year Festival was the most important religious event of the year. Here, the Babylonian story of creation would be recited, while the king acted out the story as it was told. The recitation was a 'myth', to accompany the 'ritual' carried out by the king.

3. Yet others use the term 'myth' to describe a story which expresses a truth about human life that cannot adequately be described in terms of science or history. In this sense, myth is as valid and respectable a way of thinking about life's deepest meaning as science, art, or philosophy. This is the type of 'myth' scholars have in mind when they use this term of the Genesis stories.

The trouble is that with so many possible meanings, 'myth' has become a very slippery term, and for that reason alone is unlikely to be of much help to us here. In addition, not all the stories in the early chapters of Genesis can easily be accommodated even within the three definitions of 'myth' listed above. For although many people would be happy to think of the stories of creation and the fall as a kind of 'theology in pictures', the stories of the flood and the tower of

Babel seem to have some connexion with historical events. Archaeologists have found mud deposits from a number of great floods which swept over the ancient world from 4000 BC onwards, and the description of the tower of Babel recalls towers (ziggurats) that have been unearthed in the same areas of Mesopotamia.

● **How many stories?** The conventional way of explaining these stories has been to suggest that Genesis is actually a composite document, and what we now have has been put together out of a number of sources. Old Testament scholars have often claimed to be able to distinguish not one, but two (or even more) accounts of creation and the flood. The reasons for this are more fully explained in *The Old Testament Story*, pages 152-56. But even supposing that this analysis is correct, it is difficult to see how it can help us to understand what Genesis is trying to say. To explain where an author got his materials is not the same as explaining what he wanted to say. Unless we read these stories as they are, we are unlikely to make much headway in discovering their message.

● **What kind of stories?** If we take the stories of creation and the fall, it is easy to see that the beginning of the story is quite different in character from its sequel. This is not because they are variant accounts of the same thing (as some think), but because they are different literary forms. The first section has many close similarities to the poetic style that we find in the psalms, and especially in certain passages in the book of Isaiah. It is written in poetic style, with a repetitive refrain. From a literary standpoint it is a hymn in praise of creation, celebrating God's greatness and his concern for every living thing. It takes the observable features of the world, and asserts that God is in control of them all. It is the sort of confession of faith that may well have been formulated and used in the context of worship in ancient Israel. When we come to consider its message these are the terms in which we need to try to understand it.

Genesis 1:1 — 2:4
Genesis 2:4 — 3:24

Genesis 1:1 — 2:4

Genesis 2:4 — 3:24

What follows is quite different. The dramatic action takes place in a different setting altogether. No longer is it reported in the measured language of lofty poetry, but with the directness of an expert story-teller. In a straightforward account, we read of how the man and woman who enjoyed a perfect relationship with God rejected that relationship, and chose instead to be masters of their own destiny.

Their choice was simple, but its consequences incalculable. As the story unfolds, we are soon made aware that this is no ordinary story. The garden, the trees, and the creatures are all described in superlatives, as befits the momentous implications that stem from the action. For the effects of the human action described here were not restricted to the earliest age of human existence, but were to have repercussions for men and women at all times and places. It is no coincidence that the author names the central actors Adam (meaning 'mankind') and Eve (meaning something like 'humanity'). For the experience of all subsequent generations was enshrined in their act of disobedience. Their story is theological writing at its best and most imaginative, simple yet profound. No reader with even a glimmer of aesthetic appreciation can fail to grasp what the author is saying.

The message of the stories

What then is the message of these chapters? We shall look at some specific aspects later. But the overall theme is well summed up in the refrain repeated throughout the creation hymn: 'God was pleased with what he saw.' It is not surprising that the composer of the hymn should have repeated this statement so many times. In his own day, it was distinctive enough, and it makes an emphasis that even today is often avoided by religious people. It is a basic assumption of many Eastern religions that the world as we know it – indeed, our whole bodily existence – is quite incompatible with spiritual enlightenment. Down through the centuries, this has been a dominant theme in much Christian thinking too, and has led many people to opt out of the world in the hope that by so doing they would somehow get closer to God.

Attitudes such as this within Christianity owe more to the influence of Greek philosophy than to the Bible. The Old Testament stands fundamentally opposed to this idea. Unlike the Greeks, the Israelites did not see this world as a 'prison' from which they needed to escape in order to find God. It was, rather, their home, and God was to be found not beyond the created world, but in it. One of the basic affirmations of the Old Testament faith is that 'the world and all that is in it belong to the Lord; the earth and all who live on it are his'. Moreover, the creation stories emphasize that God is directly involved with the life of this world. He is, of course, all-powerful, and his word alone is sufficient to bring his will to fruition. But in describing the place of men and women in creation, God's own personal involvement is always emphasized. He is like a potter, who takes soil from the ground and with his own hands forms a human being out of it. Unlike many of the traditional gods of the Middle East, Yahweh can never be identified with nature: he is beyond it and above it. But at the same time, he is directly involved in the work of creation, thus demonstrating his close concern not only for Israel, but for people and animals in general, and even for the very stuff out of which the universe is made.

Psalm 24:1

Genesis 1:3, 6, 9, 11, 14, 20, 24

Genesis 2:7

Genesis in its context

Just over 100 years ago, archaeologists uncovered the library of the seventh-century BC Assyrian emperor Ashurbanipal. Politically, he was a failure, but his library survived and is one of our major sources of knowledge of the Old Testament world. It was written on cuneiform tablets, which are virtually indestructible: flat bricks of river mud written on with a wedge-shaped stick while still soft, and then baked hard in the heat of the sun. The contents of these stories were ancient even in Ashurbanipal's day, and go back almost to the dawn of civilization.

It soon became apparent from these documents that stories of creation and a great flood had circulated in ancient Babylon long before the Old Testament was written. In a wave of enthusiasm for new discoveries, the scholars who first deciphered these texts concluded that the Old Testament stories were taken from them, and were therefore of relatively little value. Things have changed a lot since then, and modern experts are now far less confident that we can trace a direct line of descent from the Babylonian documents to the stories in Genesis. One of the main reasons for this has been the more recent discovery of other religious texts from the Canaanite stronghold of Ugarit. These texts tell the stories of

Baal and other Canaanite gods and goddesses, and have shown that in many crucial respects Canaanite religion was rather different from its Babylonian counterpart. Though Ugarit's heyday had passed long before there was a nation called Israel, it is still likely that the religious context in which the Old Testament developed must have had more in common with such Canaanite beliefs than with the developed religious traditions of ancient Babylon. As a result, scholars now find it far more productive to compare the Old Testament with what we know of the religion of Ugarit.

Imagery from other religions

Many ordinary readers of the Bible may feel uneasy with the idea that it contains materials connected with the documents of other religions. But in fact this kind of religious borrowing is found not only in the stories of creation and the flood, but in many other parts of the Old Testament. The wisdom books are often very similar to wisdom books found in Egypt and elsewhere, and much of Israel's case law resembles the precepts of other nations. Parallels are perhaps to be expected, for they concern matters of morality and social organization that are common to people all over the world. It is more surprising to discover that the Old Testament's religious imagery is also quite similar to the language used of other gods. As we shall see in a later chapter, the Old Testament's language of sacrifice was essentially the same as that used in Ugarit. And the psalms in particular use many concepts that were not exclusive to Israel:

● For instance, the statement that the temple hill in Jerusalem is 'in the far north' (Psalm 48:2) has puzzled many people, for Jerusalem was not in the north, but right in the middle of the country!

But the Hebrew word for 'north' is virtually identical with the Ugaritic word 'Zaphon'. In the stories of Baal Mt Zaphon is frequently mentioned as the traditional home of the gods. So when the psalmist penned these words, it is almost certain that he was not making a (false) geographical statement about the location of the temple, but was claiming that whatever was supposed to happen at Mt Zaphon was actually taking place on Mt Zion. There are other references to this home of the gods in Isaiah 14:13, and perhaps also in Psalm 89:12.

● Psalm 46:4 speaks of 'a river that brings joy to the city of God'. There is no literal river in Jerusalem, but this statement makes perfectly good sense when we learn that the same imagery was used throughout the Middle East to illustrate the life-giving powers of divine beings. In a scene from the palace at Mari, for example, the king is shown being invested by a god. In one corner stand two figures holding a vase with the tree of life, from which comes a stream, dividing into smaller streams, and so dispensing the blessing of the gods among the people. The same theme is taken up and developed further in Ezekiel 47:1–12, where the stream that flows from the temple in Jerusalem transforms the life of everything that comes in contact with it.

● In many passages celebrating God's triumphant power, he is depicted as winning battles over the sea and monsters which lived in it. Some of these passages depict unruly waters which are threatening to bring chaos into the world which he has made (Psalms 18:15; 29:3–4,10–11; 77:16–18; 93:3–4; Habakkuk 3:8). Others speak of monsters emerging from the unruly depths to challenge God's power (Job 7:12; Psalm 74:12–14; 89:10; Isaiah 27:1). These are obviously allusions to incidents that must have been well known to the people of ancient Israel. Yet the Old Testament nowhere contains a simple descriptive account of them. For that we need to look elsewhere. These references to a battle between God and the powers of the sea are drawn from the general religious ideas of the time, rather than belonging uniquely to the Old Testament faith.

Some of the closest parallels with the Old Testament statements can be found in the texts from Ugarit. When Isaiah speaks of Yahweh using 'his powerful and deadly sword to punish Leviathan, that wriggling, twisting dragon, and to kill the monster that lives in the sea' (27:1), he uses words virtually identical with a text which speaks of Baal: 'You have killed Lotan the primeval dragon, you have seen off that twisting snake, the powerful one with the seven heads.' Other Old Testament passages attest the belief that such monsters had multiple heads (Psalm 74:13–14), and that they can be called Rahab as well as Leviathan (Psalm 89:10; Isaiah 51:9).

So what are we to make of all this? After the outspoken prophetic condemnation of Canaanite religion, why does the Old Testament use this language? Was the Old Testament faith perhaps not as distinctive as we would like to think? Some have certainly

This Babylonian account of creation tells of a time when nothing existed except the gods and the great Deep. Then a movement took place in the waters and the god Marduk formed first the earth and then the living world.

suggested that, regarding this imagery as the remnants of what was once a highly developed nature mythology in which Yahweh played much the same role as the Canaanite Baal. But there is no real evidence, either historical or religious, to support such a contention (see *The Old Testament Story*, pages 89–90).

The way these materials have been adapted for Israelite use is far more subtle than that. In Middle Eastern thinking, the waters of chaos were essentially personifications of the natural forces that seemed to bring productive life to a standstill at the end of each season. But in the Old Testament, this imagery is either set very clearly in the context of God's firm control over the powers of nature (Psalm 74:12–17; 95:5; 135:5–7; Isaiah 51:15–16), or else is given a completely different reference altogether by being applied to the great events of Israel's history. In particular, the waters of chaos are often transformed into the waters of the Red Sea, controlled by Yahweh to allow his people to escape from Egypt (Psalm 77:16–18; Isaiah 51:9–11). And the monsters become symbols of the more tangible enemies with whom Israel had to deal throughout her troubled existence (as in Isaiah 27:1). In other words, the imagery has been separated altogether from its original context, and in its new setting is given a new emphasis to celebrate some of the most distinctive aspects of the Old Testament faith.

A 'Babylonian Genesis'?

The same thing has happened in the early chapters of Genesis, with the stories of creation and the flood. It is natural that here the Old Testament should have many elements in common with other texts of its day. For although the events of history were the unique possession of just one nation, the facts of creation were part of the common heritage of humanity. When the Old Testament describes the world, it does so in conventional terms. But in the process, it reinterprets these traditional ideas in such a way that they become a means of explaining its own distinctive beliefs about God.

● **The creation story** (Genesis 1:1–2:4) has often been compared with an old Akkadian tale called *Enuma Elish*. This was recited in the temple at Babylon at the annual New Year Festival, and was a hymn in praise of the god Marduk. It tells how at the beginning nothing existed except the dark waters of primeval chaos, personified as Apsu and Tiamat. In their turn they reproduce a series of other gods representing the various elements of the universe. Later, a revolt against these forces of chaos led by the younger and more active gods brought into existence the ordered world. Apsu was killed by magic, and Tiamat was cut in two. With one half of her body Marduk made the solid sky (firmament), and with the other the flat earth. The gods were then divided between heaven and earth, and people were made to perform menial tasks for the gods on earth.

It is unlikely that there was any direct connexion between this and the Old Testament account, though there are some superficial similarities. In both, light emerges from a watery chaos, followed by the sky, dry land, sun, moon and stars, and finally people. After this the creator or creators rested. There are, of course, many differences. But even at the points of closest resemblance, the Genesis account deliberately undermines the assumptions of the Babylonian story.

Scholars of an earlier generation often linked the 'raging ocean' of Genesis 1:2 (Hebrew *tehom)* with the Babylonian goddess Tiamat. This is linguistically unlikely. But in addition, the Old Testament idea of 'the raging sea' is quite different, with not the least suggestion of a conflict between God and the watery chaos. Instead, 'the power of God' was 'moving over the water' from the very beginning, and the 'great sea monsters' are explicitly said to have been only a part of what God created. The Hebrew word used to describe their creation is carefully chosen, to indicate that God's control over these creatures was quite effortless and in no way the outcome of some cosmic battle.

Nor is there any idea that this 'raging ocean' would somehow again get the upper hand and plunge things back into chaos. This was basic to the whole idea of the Babylonian stories. Genesis makes it clear that creation is not something needing to be repeated in the ritual of an annual New Year Festival. It happened once and for all. Once the days of creation were passed they could not be repeated.

Many ancient people thought the sun, moon and stars had powers over people. Many modern readers of horoscopes think the same thing, but such beliefs are quite specifically undermined here by describing the heavenly bodies as nothing more than 'lights' (Genesis 1:14–19). They were

The Babylonian myths had a story of a Great Flood, parallel in some ways to the story of Noah. It forms part of the Epic of Gilgamesh, and tells of a man whom the gods instructed to make a boat and survive a flood.

certainly not gods themselves.

The picture of people is also quite different. In many ancient stories, they were created as an afterthought to serve the gods, so they would not have to gather their own food. But in the Old Testament men and women are not only central to the whole of God's purposes: they are the pinnacle of his creation. Far from being made for God's selfish benefit, he provides other things for theirs – and so the plants and grains are available for food (Genesis 1:29). As in the rest of the Old Testament, the destiny of people is in the hands of a loving and powerful personal God, and not in the control of either nature or superstition.

● **The Flood Story** (Genesis 6:9–9:17) displays essentially the same characteristics. Neither Egyptian nor Ugaritic literature contains an account of a great flood, but again several such stories have been found in Babylon.

The most complete of these is in a poem known as *The Epic of Gilgamesh*. This tells how Gilgamesh, king of Uruk (Erech in Genesis 10:10), shattered by the death of his friend Enkidu, realizes that he himself must soon die and decides to try to find the secret of eternal life. He seeks out his own ancestor Ut-napishtim, who had himself gained immortality, and asks him about it. He is told that first he must get a plant from the bottom of the ocean which will renew his youth. But at this point in the story, Ut-napishtim goes on to tell Gilgamesh how he himself had escaped from a great flood.

He had been warned by Ea, the god of magic wisdom, that the other gods, especially Enlil, had decided to send the flood. Ut-napishtim was advised to build a boat, which he did. The 'boat' was in fact a large cube, and in important respects was therefore rather different from Noah's 'ark'. After coating this cube inside and out with bitumen, he stocked it with food and brought all his family and belongings into it, together with animals and skilled craftsmen. The storm raged for seven days, at the end of which nothing but water could be seen. Twelve days later, Ut-napishtim's 'boat' ran aground on a mountain. He sent out a dove and a swallow in turn, both of which came back. Then he sent out a raven, which did not return as the waters had subsided. When he left the 'boat', he made a sacrifice to the gods, who crowded round like flies to smell it. They promised that never again would they send a flood, and gave immortality to Ut-napishtim and his wife.

Here again, there is no compelling evidence to suggest that the Genesis story is in any way based on the Babylonian account. But there are sufficient resemblances to make it likely that both depend on the same general stock of ideas. Where they differ, they do so because the Old Testament story is based on a different understanding of the nature of God himself. In the Gilgamesh story, no explanation is given for the flood, though in another Akkadian source (the *Atrahasis Epic*), the gods decide to destroy men and women because they are making too much noise! In Genesis, however, God sends the flood as a judgment on human disobedience. Throughout the story the recurring theme is that there is only one God. Unlike the Babylonian gods he is not afraid of the flood: he is in complete control of it. Nor does he deal with men and women in an arbitrary way. The saving of Noah is as much the outcome of his own just nature as is the destruction of everyone else. The Genesis God is essentially a moral God, and his dealings with men and women depend solely on his own standards of justice and love, not on capricious self interest.

Men, women and God

Psalm 8:4

Psalm 144:4

Psalm 103:15–16

Psalm 8:5

Psalm 103:17

'What is man, that you think of him; mere man, that you care for him?' As people compare their own meagre existence with the greatness of the world around them, this question often sums up the basic problem of human existence. Why are we here? Some parts of the Old Testament emphasize the apparent insignificance of men and women, referring to life as 'a puff of wind ... a passing shadow', or 'like grass. We grow and flourish like a wild flower; then the wind blows on it, and it is gone ...' Others reflect a more positive mood, declaring that people are only a little lower than God himself, 'crowned with glory and honour'. Yet all would agree that the life of men and women finds its true fulfilment when they are living in personal fellowship with God. This is why we were made, and no matter how insignificant or powerless a person may feel, we can be sure that God is still interested in their life and experience: 'for those who honour the Lord, his love lasts for ever, and his goodness endures for all generations.' Men and women are the pinnacle and crowning glory of the world and all its affairs. In the Babylonian creation stories people were made last of all, almost as an afterthought, and always for menial duties. But the Old Testament will have none of this.

The heart of the Genesis creation stories is to be found in the simple statement that 'God created human beings, making them to be like himself' – or, as other translations put it, 'God created mankind in his own image'. When we recall that the Old Testament expressly forbids making images of God, this may come as a rather unexpected sentiment. But in the previous chapter we saw that the imagery of the Old Testament is always specific and positive, never abstract and philosophical. God is described in relation to what he does, not by reference to what he is made of. This is precisely the emphasis that is intended here. When God makes men and women 'to be like himself', he does not mean them to look like him, or to be made of the same stuff. Rather he intends them to be a kind of extension of his own personality, and a fundamental part of his own activity in the world. They are his representatives. In this claim at least three important ideas are put forward about the relationship between people, the world, and God himself:

Genesis 1:27

In relation to the earth

Genesis 1:28

Men and women are given God's blessing and told: 'Have many children, so that your descendants will live all over the earth and bring it under their control. I am putting you in charge of the fish, the birds, and all the wild animals.'

This statement has often been misunderstood, especially by modern Christians who have taken it as a licence to exploit the natural world in any way that is to their benefit. Older Bible translations may have encouraged this, by articulating God's instructions in terms of 'subduing' the earth, and 'having dominion' over its creatures. But the Genesis story implies nothing of this kind: indeed, quite the opposite. The whole point of the story is that God has made a world of order and balance out of a state of chaos. Men and women are here called upon to maintain and preserve the world

Opposite
The Genesis creation story shows humanity as both part of the created order, in harmony with nature as a whole, and also the summit of creation, responsible for the proper care of all life.

Amos 4:13; 5:8; Isaiah 45:12
Isaiah 40:26; 48:13
Psalm 104:10
Psalm 104:14–15,28–30

as God intends it to be. God has not wound the world up like a mechanical toy. He continues to be actively involved in its workings, changing night to day. He controls the sun, moon and stars, the rivers, and gives life to crops and animals. Any human activity which disrupts the life of nature is contrary to the will of God, for God intended there to be a mutual respect and service between people and the world in which they live.

Genesis 2:7

This is strikingly emphasized when Genesis depicts God as a divine potter forming a person out of the ground. There is a subtle play on words here, for the Hebrew word for man (*adam*) is very similar to that for 'ground' (*adamah*). This similarity is used here to emphasize that people are a fundamental part of the world system in which they live. Men and women are not above nature: they are a part of it, and are responsible to God for the way they care for their world and the other creatures with whom they share it. Denis Baly lucidly captures the spirit of this word-play in English: 'Man was never intended to be the proud ruler of conquered and enslaved territory ... he is human, taken from the humus, and therefore he must act with humility.'

In relation to God

An important part of the meaning of our creation 'in the image of God' is that people have a capacity for intimate relationships – with each other and with God.

Men and women are distinctive because God can and does speak to them. Though they are part and parcel of the world in which they live, that is not the only dimension in which life finds meaning. Indeed, a materialist view which tries to make sense of human existence by only analyzing the world of our senses and reason is, in biblical terms, meaningless. Being made 'in God's image' means that people are incomplete without God. They are intended for

fellowship with him, and it is this which gives meaning and direction to life. Communication with God is of vital importance to human satisfaction.

It is important to notice that by fellowship the Old Testament does not mean a kind of conventional religiosity. One of the most striking features of these early stories in Genesis is the way God comes and talks with people. He arrives in the evening to discuss with Adam and Eve the affairs of the day. This statement is not to be regarded with embarrassment as either hyperbole or exaggerated anthropomorphism. It is a moving affirmation of the fact that communication between God and people was intended to be delightful and personal, not formal and rigid. In ancient Israel, God's word came to his people through many different channels. The priest would interpret the Law (*Torah*); the wise man would give advice on everyday affairs; and the prophets most characteristically brought a direct word from God to particular situations in his people's life. But underlying all these modes of communication was the conviction that God and his people related to each other on a personal level. Like the characters in the Garden of Eden, each individual was made for direct encounter with God himself.

Genesis 3:8

In relation to each other

There are important lessons here about human relationships to the world and to God. But some of the most striking points of these stories concern relationships between human beings themselves at different levels.

● **In social relationships**, the fact that all human beings are made 'in God's image' implies that all are of equal value and importance. The Bible solves the problems of race by declaring that we all belong to the same race! Israel often found it difficult to grasp that. But the prophets were adamant that no one race was better than another, and no one group in society was of more importance than another. So far as God is concerned, all men and women are equal. Though Israel was specially privileged to receive God's Law (*Torah*), this did not mean that others had no access to God's will. However imperfectly they might have perceived it, every person knew the difference between basic issues of right and wrong just because they were made 'in God's image'.

● **In sexual relationships**, the Old Testament takes a realistic view. There is here no hint of the narrow asceticism that has often marked Christian views on sex. The idea that sexual knowledge only emerged in the context of broken relationships after the fall is clearly contradicted in Genesis. Human sexuality is an essential part of God's design for his people. And it is worth noting that procreation is not the only reason given for this. Though it is true that men and women are told to 'Have many children ...', great emphasis is laid on the fact that a sexual partner is to be 'a suitable companion'. Nor is there any suggestion here that in such a relationship one partner is intrinsically more important than the other. A man is incomplete without a woman, and it is only the two of them together who can work out the full potential of human existence. Sex is a part of God's

Genesis 1:28
Genesis 2:18

gift to men and women. But it is also something to be enjoyed and developed for its own sake – a point that is made most forcibly by the inclusion in the Old Testament of a book of erotic love poems, the Song of Solomon.

●**In family relationships**, there is again an emphasis on the mutual sharing of one person with another. In the Old Testament world, the patriarchal family was the norm. Men as well as women were often seen as chattels to be disposed of to suit the head of the family. The Old Testament itself gives many examples of family heads doing just that. But here in this basic exposition of God's plan we find a rather different emphasis. There is nothing here that would give grounds for the exploitation of one sex by the other. Instead, there is a very strong emphasis on the mutual commitment of men and women to each other in the context of a sexual relationship. Moreover, this relationship takes precedence over all other traditional family commitments. The book of Genesis issues a very strong challenge to the ancient supremacy of the family patriarch when it states that 'a man leaves his father and mother and is united to his wife, and they become one ...'

Genesis 2:24

Broken relationships and new beginnings

The book of Genesis paints an idyllic picture of life in this world, with nature, people and God all working together in perfect harmony and mutual understanding and support. But, of course, life is not like that. Though most people have on occasion glimpsed the idealistic possibilities that are presented here, human experience is more often marred by exploitation, disharmony, and suspicion. The real world is a world of broken relationships.

The root of the problem

Genesis 3:1–24
Genesis 11:1–9

So what has gone wrong? Two stories here answer that question: the story of the fall, and the story of the Tower of Babel. Both of them declare that the reason for human misery is that the delicate balance between people, nature and God has been disturbed. Instead of being content to accept God's will, men and women have tried to set themselves up as controllers of their own destiny. They are not content to accept even the benign guidance of a power greater than themselves. Instead, their chief concern has been to 'make a name for ourselves' or, as the story of the fall puts it, to 'be like God'.

Genesis 11:4
Genesis 3:4

One story expresses this as seeking after the fruit of 'the tree that gives knowledge of what is good and what is bad'. The fact that God bans the human pair from eating this fruit has suggested to some that there was a built-in unfairness in God's original design. After all, why should God want people to be kept in ignorance like this? But a comment like that misses the point. For elsewhere in the Old Testament, the same term is used with a distinctive connotation. To be ignorant of the difference between right and wrong indicates that a person is yet a child, depending for guidance and direction on his or her parents. In the case of a child, of course, it is important that they grow up and eventually gain independence from their parents. But in a person's relationship with God this can never happen. To

Genesis 2:17; 3:4–5

Deuteronomy 1:39; Isaiah 7:14–15

have a meaningful relationship with God, men and women must be prepared to recognize his greatness and love, and relate to him as a child to a generous parent.

People who do not have a childlike trust in God are in revolt against their Creator. God has given limits within which life can prosper. When human selfishness tries to overstep these limits, disaster will soon follow. One of the most moving aspects of these stories is the contrast between the world as God intended it to be and the world of broken relationships so familiar to us all. The Bible's understanding of the nature of sin at this point is, of course, quite different from the view taken by many people today. It is often assumed that the history of the human race is one long story of continuous improvement, as people moved from primitive and savage beginnings to the so-called sophistication of our own day. Christians adopt various positions on the question of biological evolution. But there can be no argument about the possibility of moral evolution. The facts of history prove conclusively that people are getting worse, not better. Genesis explains it by saying that human life has moved from a position of fellowship with God to a position of rebellion. And it traces it all back to the disobedience of the man and woman in Eden who knew God so well.

The results of their disobedience and selfishness are simple:

Genesis 3:14–21

● **Disharmony in nature** Mutual service and interdependence between people and the natural world is replaced by hostility and mutual distrust.

Genesis 3:8–10
Genesis 3:22–24

● **Alienation from God** Instead of meeting God in a close personal relationship, the man and woman avoid him, and are ultimately sent out of the garden.

The charter for family life laid down in the creation story is of a marriage of equals, bringing different attributes into a partnership. Within this setting children find their secure place.

Genesis 4:1–16

● **Broken society** With broken relationships between people, the world and God, even brothers can become enemies – and so Cain goes out and kills his brother Abel.

Searching for the answer

The people of Israel knew well enough what all this meant in the ordinary details of everyday life. By the time these stories were finally written down, they could look back on a long history which amply illustrated the tragedy of human disobedience. But they had also learned that even when his judgment was well deserved, God could never leave people to languish in the results of their own sin. These early stories contain a vivid portrayal of broken relationships. But

A spoiled creation

People's good relations with each other
in marriage and the family, in social harmony and co-operation . . .

. . . are broken by human sinfulness,
so that marriages break up, social and racial divisions arise, and wars kill millions

People's good relations with the land,
so that by caring for the created world and sharing its resources we can all have enough . . .

. . . are broken by human greed,
resulting in plenty for some, deprivation for others, and a polluted world

People's good relations with God,
in direct awareness of him, and in worshipping him as he really is . . .

. . . are broken by human pride,
so that we have a distorted understanding of God, and worship the creation rather than the Creator

they also have an underlying emphasis on the ever-present possibility of a new beginning. Sin and disobedience are a tragedy. Judgment is inevitable – and well deserved. But God's love and forgiveness for the world and its people will never be defeated.

Even in the earliest stories there are hints that God cannot just abandon people. When Adam and Eve feel the need for clothing, God provides it for them. When Cain kills his brother Abel, God condemns him – but then forgives him and takes steps to keep him safe from the vengeance of others. This theme comes to full expression in the story of the great flood. At a time when men and women were so determined to go their own way and disturb the delicate balance of relationships between God and his world, judgment was the only possible answer. Yet even here, God's purpose is not ultimately destructive, and Noah is saved. He is spared because of God's love, grace, and forgiveness – all of which is encapsulated in the promise freely given by God to all humanity. The rainbow, given at that time, is a sign of his continuing love even through the worst excesses of human disobedience.

It is little wonder then that these stories came to form the opening pages of the Old Testament. In them we have a profound and picturesque summary of all the essential features of the Old Testament faith. Here we meet a God who is both totally different from men and women, and yet deeply involved with them. We are given a glimpse of a world in which people and nature can relate meaningfully to each other, because both of them relate to God. And we see the tragic results when that relationship breaks down.

The tragedy is familiar enough to us all. But the Old Testament has its own diagnosis of the problem. The world is out of joint because men and women are in revolt against their Creator. Human sin affects both human life and the life of nature. Disobedience is a tragedy, and wilful neglect of God's will leads to judgment. The

Genesis 3:21

Genesis 4:15

Genesis 6:5–8

Genesis 9:8–17

The story of humanity's fall into sin speaks of a breakdown in relationships at every level. There is evidence of this breakdown throughout history, particularly in the cruelty and waste of wars.

The task God gave humanity, of working for the good of the whole living world, can only be achieved through co-operation. Sinfulness shatters that co-operation and brings bitter hostility.

course of human history has demonstrated all this often enough. But the Old Testament does not leave it there. For God wishes to bring order out of this chaos. He intends to replace alienation with healing. And his forgiveness and love are always available to those who in childlike simplicity acknowledge their dependence on the Creator.

Looking to the future

The Old Testament clearly asserts that human existence finds its true fulfilment only in a close personal relationship with God. But where are the boundaries of that relationship to be drawn? Does it end with death – or does it extend further, into an after-life?

To modern people this is a natural question to ask. For one thing, we tend to think of people as individuals rather than as a part of some much larger group, and the fate of each person is therefore of considerable importance to us. In addition, we have been nurtured in an environment where popular ideas about death often incorporate the ancient Greek view that a person is composed of two parts: a body, which is mortal and comes to an end, and a soul (or spirit) which is immortal and can last for ever quite independently of the body.

Neither of these assumptions would have meant very much in the Old Testament context. Although we should not over-emphasize the corporate aspect of Old Testament thought it is certainly true that ancient Israel thought

far less in terms of the individual than we do. And at the same time, the Old Testament contains not a trace of the bipartite view of human nature that leads to the conclusion that people are souls imprisoned in bodies. For the Old Testament writers, all aspects of human existence were just different facets of the same reality. Though it was possible to speak of a person's 'heart', or even 'spirit', terms of this sort did not refer to independent entities, but were only a graphic way of describing a person's emotions and general motivation. A person's bodily existence could in no way be distinguished from other aspects of the human experience.

With such an outlook, death is simply taken for granted as part of the whole business of human existence. It may be regrettable, but is a perfectly natural thing (2 Samuel 14:14), and there is nothing anyone can do about it (Job 7:9; Psalm 89:48). Two of the great heroes of the Old Testament story – Joshua and David – express the general view in their final speeches: 'I am about to go the way of all the earth' (Joshua 23:14;

The Israelites set great store by the continuance of the family name in future generations.

Old Testament people accepted death as a natural part of life. But are there some hints of belief in life hereafter?

1 Kings 2:2). The author of Psalm 90 defines the human life span as 'seventy years ... eighty years, if we are strong' (Psalm 90:10). With characteristic coolness the author of Ecclesiastes states that 'For everything there is a season, and a time for every matter under heaven: a time to be born, and a time to die ...' (3:1–2). And when the time comes, 'No one can keep himself from dying or put off the day of his death. That is a battle we cannot escape ...' (8:8). Even if we try to understand it, 'no one can tell us what will happen after we die' (Ecclesiastes 10:14; 3:22). Of course, Ecclesiastes has its own cynical viewpoint, and we need to make allowances for that in reading these passages. But when we look to the rest of the Old Testament, comments of this sort are not altogether inappropriate. For although many Old Testament passages seem to allude to the continued survival of dead people, there is no consistent picture. We can trace a number of different emphases in the Old Testament:

● At a popular level, it seems likely that many ordinary people shared much of the superstition of the ancient Middle East. Egyptians and Babylonians, as well as the people of Ugarit in Canaan, all believed that there was another life after death. The Egyptians made the most elaborate preparations for the comfort of the deceased in this new environment, and it was widely believed that the dead should be given sufficient provisions to ensure a comfortable life. Tombs discovered at Ugarit were equipped with channels through which living worshippers could pour food and drink

to their dead ancestors. Such offerings were often motivated by the view that the dead could influence the lives of the living, and if they were kept well fed then their influence would be good rather than evil. The Old Testament provides evidence for similar attitudes in Israel. The most striking instance of this is Saul's belief that the dead Samuel could somehow affect the course of his own life (1 Samuel 28:3–19). Saul was roundly condemned for this – and other Old Testament passages condemn similar reverence for the dead as alien to the true Old Testament faith (Deuteronomy 26:14; Ezekiel 43:7–9; Isaiah 8:19–20; 65:1–5).

● A more orthodox view suggested that a person could in some way survive through the continuation of their family line. This assumption seems to lie behind the book of Ruth, and is hinted at in many passages which suggest that a person who dies without children to preserve the family is at a particular disadvantage.

● The most common description of the dead is that they live a shadowy, indeterminate existence in a place called Sheol. Sheol is not to be confused with later Christian ideas of heaven and hell. It is a morally neutral term, and what actually goes on in Sheol is never really made clear. Sometimes, existence there is spoken of as an imprisonment, with those who are there isolated from God and completely unaware of anything (Psalm 30:9; 88:10–12; 115:17; Job 14:20–22; Ecclesiastes 9:5–6). At other times, God's power is said to extend even to Sheol (Amos 9:2; Psalm 139:8), but these sentiments are essentially poetic and rhetorical. They are meant to encourage the living rather than to make definitive statements about the state of the dead.

● Yet other Old Testament passages have been taken to refer to the idea of resurrection from the dead. There is only one absolutely clear statement of belief in a resurrection, and that is Daniel 12:2. Because of this it is often supposed that the idea of resurrection was a relative latecomer in the Old Testament faith, articulated at a time when the deaths of good people were especially hard to accept (for the circumstances surrounding Daniel, see *The Old Testament Story*, pages 174–87). But this is difficult to sustain, and it is more likely that the idea of resurrection emerged naturally from a much earlier period. Some of the oldest poetry in the Old Testament seems to imply resurrection (Deuteronomy 32:39;

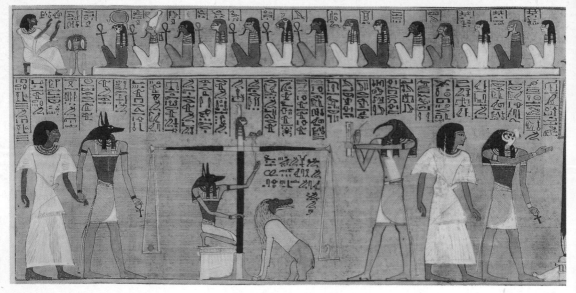

The Egyptians certainly believed in life after death. In this papyrus a man's heart is being weighed against a feather, as he prepares for his final journey.

1 Samuel 2:6), and there are three stories of resurrections from the dead told in the Deuteronomistic History (1 Kings 17:8–24; 2 Kings 4:8–37; 13:20–21). Though these stories raise other questions, the way they are told suggests that their readers would be familiar with the possibility of resurrection from the dead. The same can also be said about other passages, for instance, Hosea 6:1–3, Ezekiel 37:1–14, Isaiah 53:8–12, and Job 19:25–27. Some scholars have also argued that the references to Sheol could at least imply resurrection. Existence there is characterized as a sleep in silence and darkness – and in Daniel, resurrection is referred to as an awakening from the sleep of death.

It certainly seems likely that this later articulation of a resurrection belief emerged from the earlier faith of Israel, rather than coming in from some other source, as was once believed. We know that it was the subject of continual argument for a very long time. Even in the time of the New Testament, the Sadducees still could not bring themselves to accept that resurrection of the dead was an authentic part of the Old Testament faith. The Pharisees, and probably most ordinary Jewish people, took a different view. But we should notice that, where the Old Testament does mention resurrection it is essentially the reversal of physical death, and the restoration of the life in this world that was there before. The idea that resurrection life could have a distinctive and different quality is not found in the Old Testament. Nor is the belief that resurrection signified the defeat of death. Both those developments were to come later, and grew out of the Christian belief in the resurrection of Jesus.

4 God and his people

THE OLD Testament faith emerged from the corporate history of Israel's people. This meant it could be tested in the affairs of everyday life. It was not a series of abstract speculations about God. Though Israel's theologians were constantly questioning and refining their understanding of God and his ways, their faith was never merely an intellectual process. At the centre of the Old Testament faith is a relationship between God and his people. Israel's faith and Israel's style of life could not be separated. How then, in practical terms, did God and his people relate to one another?

Belief and behaviour

It seems to be almost endemic within human nature that people express their deepest convictions in those special forms of behaviour that we would normally call 'organized religion'. Israel was no exception. Worship at the local and national sanctuaries took place in strictly defined circumstances, and included a wide variety of activities. Prayer, praise, sacrifice – all these things were just as typical of the Old Testament faith as they are of many other religions. When Israelite people met for organized worship, they were expressing their appreciation for all that God had done for them.

We shall leave this aspect of the Old Testament faith until later. For in the Old Testament, a person's response to God was always intended to be much broader than that. Many writers emphasized

The life of the market-place was never intended to be distinct from the life of worship. Repeatedly the prophets condemned a religiosity which made no difference to everyday behaviour.

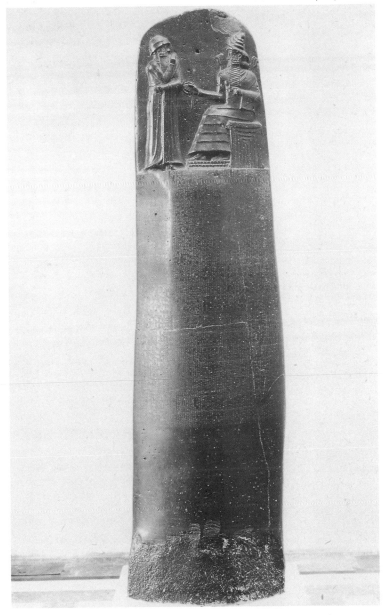

The law-code of King Hammurabi of Babylon is inscribed on this column (or *stele*). This ancient code bears a considerable likeness to some Old Testament laws.

that what went on in the shrine must never be separated from the way people lived day by day in the market-place, on the farm or at home. The prophet Micah was outspoken in condemning the empty performance of religious rituals, and emphasized that true worship of God was quite different and far more demanding: 'the Lord has told us what is good. What he requires of us is this: to do what is just, to show constant love, and to live in humble fellowship with our God.' Most of the prophets made similar statements. So too did the history writers, as well as the poets and the wisdom teachers.

Micah 6:8
1 Samuel 15:22
Psalm 51:16–17
Proverbs 21:3

God had shown by his actions in history and nature that his love and concern extend to every area of human life. So too, every aspect of Israel's experience was to be affected by their commitment to him. The relationship between God and his people was to have a moral, as well as a cultic basis. The nation's response to God must be shown in the way they behaved, not just in what they believed.

This conviction runs deeply throughout the Old Testament. Even those books which relate to the formalities of organized worship are founded on moral and spiritual values. At the heart of the book of Deuteronomy is the instruction to 'Love the Lord your God with all your heart, with all your soul, and with all your strength'. Love for neighbours is also advocated in another section of Old Testament Law – and it is notable that the Ten Commandments sum up Israel's duty to God predominantly in terms of social and personal morality.

Deuteronomy 6:5

Leviticus 19:18
Exodus 20:1–17; Deuteronomy 5:6–22

At one time, scholars imagined that this emphasis on behaviour was a late development within the Old Testament faith. Many nineteenth-century thinkers believed that the sort of biological

These pillars of salt in the Dead Sea are close to a possible site for Sodom and Gomorrah. This early story shows a deep concern that religion and morality should go together.

evolution popularized by Charles Darwin had been paralleled by a moral and spiritual evolution, as human attitudes had developed and matured. Theories such as this encouraged people to take it for granted that Israel's religious experience must have begun as a simple nature worship, which only evolved into high moral standards under the influence of great thinkers such as the Old Testament prophets, who tried to persuade their people to move from superstition to a more sophisticated understanding of God and his ways.

This sort of view of the Old Testament faith has had many supporters. But it is simplistic and superficial:

● The whole concept of evolutionary philosophy has now been discredited. The idea that people began in primitive savagery and are getting better all the time simply does not square with the facts. The violence and brutality of our own generation makes it perfectly obvious that people are not improving. The madness of the nuclear arms race suggests they might even be getting worse.

● In the last seventy-five years, our knowledge of the ancient world in general, and of Israel's neighbours in particular, has changed considerably. Earlier scholars did not have the benefit of these insights, and it was correspondingly difficult for them to understand the Old Testament in its own true life setting. We now know that some aspects of Old Testament morality were familiar to people throughout the ancient Middle East. Much of Israel's civil law in particular bears a close resemblance to concepts of justice going back at least as far as the law code of King Hammurabi of Babylon (about 1700 BC).

● Literary analysis of the Old Testament stories has shown that a concern for good behaviour is central to many of the oldest traditions. The story of the destruction of Sodom and Gomorrah is

The Old Testament books of Wisdom instruct the rich to have a care for the poor.

The Book of Proverbs is full of concern for children to be wisely brought up in a secure family environment.

Genesis 18:16–33

Exodus 2:11–13

certainly much older than the time of the prophets – and yet it condemns immorality in no uncertain terms. The stories about Moses also go back to ancient sources, and show his anger at moral injustices as they affected both himself and his people.

● The Old Testament law codes themselves contain instructions about the conduct of religious services alongside clear instructions about maintaining a just society. Such references were once dismissed as later additions to bring the laws into line with the message of the prophets. But further study has shown that even the very earliest strands of the Old Testament's legal material emphasize the importance of everyday behaviour as a way of serving God.

Exodus 23:1–9; Deuteronomy 16:18–20; Leviticus 19:15–18

Everyday behaviour was always a crucial factor in the Old Testament faith. But even today, religious people the world over know how easy it is to depend on the performance of familiar rituals as a means of trying to please God. Israel was no different. When the great prophets reminded them that faith in God should affect the whole of life, this was no new revelation: it was the recalling of the people back to the ideals of their ancient covenant faith.

Discovering God's will

What exactly were these ideals – and how were they expressed in terms of everyday life? There are two main sections of the Old Testament where we can find the answer to these questions: the wisdom books; and the books of Law (Genesis to Deuteronomy), supplemented by the messages of the prophets.

The Wisdom books
Against Apion I.8

The Jewish historian Josephus (first century AD) described the wisdom books as 'precepts for the conduct of human life'. There are three of these books in the Old Testament: Proverbs, Ecclesiastes and Job. Josephus was probably thinking especially of the book of

Proverbs, which contains many memorable observations on how people should behave in order to enjoy a satisfying life. Here we find advice of the sort that parents throughout the world might give to their children. Many of the instructions of the book of Proverbs would not have been out of place in quite different cultural contexts. Indeed, one whole section of Proverbs is at many points identical with an Egyptian document of about the twelfth century BC, the *Teaching of Amenemope.*

Proverbs 22:17 — 23:11

Understanding 'wisdom'

In the ancient world, the pursuit of 'wisdom' seems to have involved many different skills. Sometimes a 'wise' person was a good diplomat; at other times, a person with specialist knowledge about the world and its workings – perhaps a botanist or zoologist. When Solomon prayed for 'wisdom', he asked to be given the ability 'to rule ... with justice and to know the difference between good and evil'. But he could also be called a 'wise man' because of his literary and artistic interests.

1 Kings 4:33

1 Kings 3:9

1 Kings 4:32

'Wisdom' was obviously a very wide-ranging series of skills. Perhaps it was a term used simply to denote the possession of whatever abilities were necessary for a particular individual to be successful in their own sphere of life. For some, that meant technical training in the art of international relations. Israel no doubt had schools attached to the royal courts where this kind of formal education would be given. For others, it meant the study of science and philosophy – a sort of ancient university education. But for most, it meant the cultivation of those personal qualities that would result in happy and meaningful relationships in the everyday life of home and work-place.

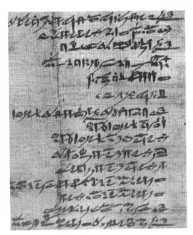

There were 'wisdom' traditions in some of Israel's neighbouring cultures. The *Teaching of Amenemope,* an Egyptian document, is quoted almost verbatim in a section of Proverbs.

Deuteronomy 6:6–7

Nowadays, most people learn these social skills in school. There is some evidence that the Canaanite city-states had a formal education system. But in Israel, the family was the main influence in the life of a growing child. Young people would learn most of what they needed to know from their parents, grandparents, and the village elders. The practice recommended in the book of Deuteronomy almost certainly continued through most of the Old Testament period: 'Never forget these commands that I am giving you today. Teach them to your children. Repeat them when you are at home and when you are away, when you are resting and when you are working ...'

Wisdom in practice

The Old Testament wisdom books contain examples of all these different kinds of 'wisdom'. Job and Ecclesiastes are the product of a well-developed intellectual approach to the great imponderables of human existence: the problem of evil, and the apparent meaninglessness of so much of life. As such, they do not tell us much in a direct way about everyday behaviour in ancient Israel – though they do, of course, take certain moral standards for granted. In the book of Proverbs we find a much greater emphasis on 'practical wisdom'. Yet even here, there seems to be a good deal of interest in scientific study, for moral lessons are often reinforced and illustrated by reference to the life of the animals and events in the natural world.

The book of Proverbs is itself an anthology of materials emanating from various wisdom teachers. But its contents are remarkably consistent, and deal with personal relationships in a number of different contexts.

The family

It is not surprising that this should be a basic concern in Proverbs, since many of its precepts almost certainly originated in the context of advice handed on from one generation to another.

As elsewhere in the Old Testament, a stable sexual relationship between husband and wife is seen as the key to family stability. Adultery is singled out as a particularly destructive evil whose repercussions affect more than the two individuals involved: 'A man can hire a prostitute for the price of a loaf of bread, but adultery will cost him all he has.' As we might expect in view of what we have already seen in the Old Testament creation stories, wisdom teachers in Israel spoke frankly and freely about both the attractions and perils of sexual unfaithfulness: 'The lips of another man's wife may be as sweet as honey, and her kisses as smooth as olive-oil, but when it is all over, she leaves you nothing but bitterness and pain.' But the advice is never narrow-minded or prudish. The love poems in the Song of Solomon have a number of connexions with the wisdom books, and the way they depict a developing sexual relationship has often alarmed modern Christian readers by its frankness. But the same open and joyful acknowledgment of human sexuality as part of God's creation is found also in the everyday advice of the book of Proverbs. For at the same time as its readers are warned against the dangers of adultery, they are also encouraged to develop and renew relationships within the marriage context: '... be happy with your wife and find your joy with the girl you married ... Let her charms keep you happy; let her surround you with her love ...'

Proverbs 6:26

Proverbs 5:3–4

Proverbs 5:18–19

Out of a happy marriage will come happy children – and the responsibility for bringing them up is to be shared between husband and wife. Indeed, the guidance of growing children is one of the major themes of Proverbs. Such guidance should be positive, by both example and precept, aiming to 'Teach a child how he should live, and he will remember it all his life'. Even when parents need to correct their child, that should always be done from a concern to promote moral maturity in the family: 'If you don't punish your son, you don't love him. If you do love him, you will correct him.' If the right course is followed in all these matters, then the whole family will be able to share in the mutual joy of a developing relationship in which 'Old men are proud of their grandchildren, just as boys are proud of their fathers'.

Proverbs 1:8–9; 6:20–23

Proverbs 22:6

Proverbs 13:24

Proverbs 17:6

● **Friends** Next to a good family, a person needs good friends and neighbours. In practice, a friend can often be more valuable than members of the family: 'Do not forget your friends or your father's friends. If you are in trouble, don't ask your brother for help; a neighbour near by can help you more than a brother who is far away.' Of course, in order to acquire friends we need to show ourselves to be friendly: 'Never tell your neighbour to wait until tomorrow if you

Proverbs 27:10

Proverbs 3:28
Proverbs 25:17

Proverbs 26:18–19, 24
Proverbs 18:8; 26:22

Proverbs 6:16–19

Proverbs 26:5

can help him now.' We also need tact: 'Don't visit your neighbour too often; he may get tired of you and come to hate you.' Above all, a relationship between friends needs to be based on honesty: 'A hypocrite hides his hatred behind flattering words ... A man who misleads someone and then claims that he was only joking is like a madman playing with a deadly weapon.' Gossip, then as now, was one of the commonest threats to wholesome friendship. Indeed, the way people speak to each other is one of the major themes of the wisdom literature. A slogan in one of the early chapters of Proverbs sums up 'seven things that the Lord hates'– and most of them are related to the way people speak: 'A proud look, a lying tongue, hands that kill innocent people, a mind that thinks up wicked plans, feet that hurry off to do evil, a witness who tells one lie after another, and a man who stirs up trouble among friends.'

Those who behave like this are the opposite of 'wise': they are fools. And there is only one way to deal with them: 'Give a silly answer to a silly question and the one who asked it will realize that he's not as clever as he thinks.' The wise person, on the other hand, is characterized by prudent thought and speech: 'Be careful how you think; your life is shaped by your thoughts. Never say anything that isn't true ...'

● **Society** Wisdom teachers were not only concerned with the

Old Testament laws are strongly concerned for the disadvantaged, especially widows and orphans, whose care should be taken over by the whole community.

behaviour of people in small groups: they also gave much teaching on how society as a whole should operate. At the very beginning of the book of Proverbs, we learn that its advice 'can teach you how to live intelligently and how to be honest, just, and fair'. Honesty, justice and fairness in society were among the key themes in the preaching of the prophets – and they are just as important here. We may find this somewhat surprising, for most scholars are agreed that the wisdom books must have originated in fairly well-to-do circles. The fact that the wisdom teachers of Israel had international connexions supports that assumption, for wealth is required to make and sustain worldwide contacts of this kind. We certainly know that later Jewish wisdom teachers must have been quite rich. Writing about 180 BC, the wise man Ben Sirach tells of his wide travels, and gives advice on such things as behaviour at banquets and how to treat servants. He also mentions the large fees that he charged for tuition at his school! In the Old Testament itself, the description of Job certainly suggests that the authors of that book moved in high-class circles. Even in Proverbs, some pieces of advice suggest a context of relative affluence.

Proverbs 1:3

Ecclesiasticus 34:9–12
Ecclesiasticus 31:12 — 32:13
Ecclesiasticus 33:24–31
Ecclesiasticus 51:23–28

Job 1:1–3

Proverbs 21:14

It is therefore all the more surprising to find here a morality which recognizes the limitations of wealth. 'Wisdom' itself is more important than riches. So is 'peace of mind' and 'a good reputation' – all of which suggests that it is 'Better to be poor and fear the Lord than to be rich and in trouble. Better to eat vegetables with people you love than to eat the finest meat where there is hate.' The other Old Testament wisdom books make exactly the same points. Even the pessimistic author of Ecclesiastes declares that amassing money is pointless: 'It was like chasing the wind – of no use at all.' And the book of Job asserts quite bluntly that trust in money is incompatible with a living relationship to God himself: 'I have never trusted in riches or taken pride in my wealth ... Such a sin would be punished by death; it denies Almighty God.'

Proverbs 3:13–15
Proverbs 17:1
Proverbs 22:1

Proverbs 15:16–17

Ecclesiastes 2:11

Job 31:24–28

The imagery of the wisdom books may be less picturesque and dramatic than the words of the prophets, but their social perspective is remarkably similar. Many of the abuses condemned by the wisdom teachers were the same as those that caused so much concern to the prophets: unjust business practices, bribery, and taking advantage of people by charging interest on loans – all of it summed up in the slogan that it is 'Better to be poor and honest than rich and dishonest.' On a positive note, the wisdom literature is full of instructions to those who are rich to share what they have with the poor – whether it be sharing access to their land and crops, or giving them clothes, or just general exhortations to be generous to others. As elsewhere in the Old Testament, this generosity is to apply especially to those with no other visible means of support – which in ancient Israel meant especially widows and orphans. And even animals were to be treated with due concern for their welfare.

Proverbs 11:1
Proverbs 15:27
Proverbs 28:8

Proverbs 28:6

Proverbs 13:23
Job 31:19–20
Proverbs 14:21, 31

Proverbs 23:10–11; Job 31:16–18
Proverbs 14:4

Besides charity, the wisdom books also advocate justice. It is one thing to give freely to those who are poor. But social justice is a more basic human need. The wisdom books are conscious that it is people

Proverbs 30:13–14

Proverbs 31:8–9

(usually rich people) who actually create divisions within society. So they advocate a positive effort to correct social injustices: 'Speak up for people who cannot speak for themselves. Protect the rights of all who are helpless. Speak for them and be a righteous judge. Protect the rights of the poor and needy.'

Here, in the wisdom books, we have much clear guidance on how God's people should behave. Morality, like charity, was to begin at home. But its effects went wider than the individual person: they were as broad as society itself.

Wisdom and faith

The law-keeping aspect of Old Testament faith has survived into modern Judaism. This boy wears the phylactery, a box fixed to his forehead in which are copies of a part of the law.

People have often thought that the wisdom books present a different message from the prophets or the Old Testament laws. The main strands of the Old Testament faith emphasize God's actions in the life of his people, whereas the wisdom books are said to be more 'secular', based not on God's revelation of himself but on human reason. In addition, it is often asserted that whereas the prophets and lawgivers of ancient Israel were concerned with the shape of society, the wisdom books are concerned more with personal morality. We can certainly agree that some features of these books seem to justify such observations:

● They are part of an international way of thinking, and as such have a number of similarities with literature from both Babylon and Egypt. They are not, therefore, unique to Israel, and in that sense cannot be said to be exclusively based on the unique aspects of the Old Testament faith.

● They rarely, if ever, refer directly to the great events of the Old Testament story. Instead, their teaching tends to be based on commonsense and on observation of the world of nature.

Some scholars have thought of the wisdom books and their moral teaching as a secular, humanistic intrusion into the Old Testament faith. They regard them as the religious side of those social and political changes that accompanied the institutionalization of the monarchy in ancient Israel, and the adoption of a lifestyle suited to the world of international politics.

But this is too simple an analysis.

Is wisdom secular?

To say that the wisdom books are 'secular' is imposing modern ways of thinking on the ancient world. Certainly, the wisdom writers take their starting-point from human experience of life. But in the ancient world in general, this was never 'humanistic' in the sense of being purely secular and non-religious. Throughout the ancient world, 'wisdom' was always based on an understanding of how the world works – but it was everywhere taken for granted that the world only worked at all because of the intentions of the gods or, in the case of the Old Testament, of one all-powerful God. To refuse to take account of this was something that only a 'fool' would do. A really wise person would never forget that even the ordinary world of everyday experience was sustained by God himself. Even a pessimist like the author of Ecclesiastes, who frankly confesses that he sometimes finds it hard to discover God at work in the world, nevertheless takes his existence for granted as a fundamental part of his view of life. Other writers were more positive: 'To be wise you must first obey the Lord... If you know the Holy One, you have understanding' (Proverbs 9:10).

Wisdom and natural law

In view of the importance the Old Testament attaches to the relationship of God and his world, it is not surprising that contemplation of the way the world is should lead to personal encounter with God himself. If, as the writer of the first few chapters of Genesis suggests, God can be found in the realities of the natural world, then it is hardly surprising that the discerning moralist can discover there God's demands of his people. This kind of 'natural law' is a widespread phenomenon. Even today, questions relating to human rights are often decided on the basis of some notion of 'natural justice' rather than by appeals to standards handed down from God or anyone else. The Old Testament wisdom books often appeal to precisely this sort of argument. Job, for example, asks for justice for himself because he has been just to his servants – and 'The same God who created me created my servants also' (Job 31:15).

Scholars have sometimes supposed that this sort of appeal to 'natural justice' is unique to the wisdom books. But in fact it is found throughout the Old Testament. When the prophet Amos denounces the war crimes of the nations of his day, he does so on the basis of natural justice (Amos 1:1–2:3). When the writer of Genesis condemns murder, he does it because people were made 'in God's image' (Genesis 9:6). And when Isaiah complains about the disobedience of his people, he concludes that their behaviour is unnatural and irrational because it is so different from the way that things work in the world of nature (Isaiah 1:2–3).

Apart from specific examples such as these, much of the imagery of the messages of the Old Testament prophets is also drawn from the world of nature – just as is the imagery in books such as Proverbs. At one time it was fashionable to think that the prophets had 'borrowed' ideas from the wisdom teachers. But it is much more likely that both of them were independently basing their teaching on the clear 'creation theology' of the Old Testament faith.

Wisdom and social ethics

It has also been claimed that a 'wisdom' morality is inconsistent with an emphasis on social justice. It is certainly true that teaching on the shape of society is presented more forcibly by the prophets and lawgivers in relation to the great themes of Israel's salvation history. But we do an injustice to the wise men of ancient Israel to suppose that they were interested only in themselves. Indeed, in the wider wisdom literature of the ancient world, social justice was a major concern. Protecting the poor and disadvantaged members of society was a major theme in Babylonian and Egyptian literature, as well as in the texts from Ugarit which tell of Canaanite kings showing the same sort of consideration. At the very beginning of the Old Testament book of Proverbs, its aims are summed up as teaching people 'how to live intelligently and how to be honest, just, and fair' (1:3). And the hero of the book of Job is a perfect example of a person who always did the right thing by those less fortunate than himself (Job 31:13–23). Questions about social justice are certainly a major concern of both prophets and history writers in the Old Testament. They emphasized that the shape of society should reflect God's dealings with his people. The wisdom books give different reasons for promoting equality and justice – but their ethical stance is none the less 'religious' for that.

Wisdom and the covenant

In point of fact, the actual ethical advice of the wisdom writers is often identical to the lessons of Israel's history. Caring for the poor, consideration for animals, justice in society, concern for orphans, as well as prohibition of false witness, adultery, bribery and vengeance – all of these things are as common in the wisdom literature as they are in the Old Testament laws. Indeed, the wisdom writers often express these ideas more concretely by showing how they relate to specific situations in the life of the family or the community. Time and time again, the wisdom writers apply the same lessons as the prophets and others who stood in the 'covenant' tradition. For they were all consciously serving the same God – a God whose will could be made known to his people in both the created world and the great unrepeatable events of history.

The Law

The wisdom books reflect the standards of decent behaviour that ordinary people might take for granted. But in any organized society, this kind of moral consensus needs to be clearly defined, and this is what we find in the Old Testament law books.

The first five books of the Old Testament, from Genesis to Deuteronomy, were often referred to simply as 'the Law'. Much of the material in these books is not at all like the kind of law most people would be familiar with today. Genesis in particular is a collection of stories, which at first sight we might expect to be regarded as some sort of history. But the Old Testament notion of 'law' was much more comprehensive and wide-ranging than ours. When we talk of 'the law' we generally have in mind sets of rules that can be interpreted by lawyers with special professional training, and applied in a court of justice by a judge. It would certainly be unusual for a modern person to agree with one of the Old Testament poets who wrote, 'I take pleasure in your law'.

Psalm 119:77

But the Hebrew word for law *(Torah)* meant far more than just rules and regulations. It really included everything that God had revealed to his people – but especially the 'guidance' or 'instruction' that he would give to their lives. In the Old Testament, the Law is the place to discover what people can believe about God, and what he requires of them in return. This is why the *Torah* is so closely bound up with the stories of Israel's early history. Knowing and obeying God is not just a matter of blind obedience to religious and moral rules: it is a question of experiencing God's concern and love in a personal and social context. God's undeserved love to his people – shown in events such as the exodus – is basic to the Old Testament laws. Israel did not keep the Law in order to become God's people, but because they were already living in a close relationship to him.

The German scholar Albrecht Alt believed that some of the Old Testament's most distinctive laws emerged in this way out of Israel's experience of God. Many Old Testament laws are similar to laws in other ancient societies, for they concern the everyday happenings of rural life. Alt called these 'casuistic' or case laws – laws in which very specific situations were envisaged, and guidance given as to how disputes may be resolved. A typical law of this kind might deal with violent assault, or with the processes of responsible farming.

Exodus 21:20
Exodus 22:6

But the Old Testament also contains other, more absolute regulations, such as the Ten Commandments, where worship of other gods, murder, adultery, theft, lying and adultery are all prohibited without any further qualification or explanation. Moreover, such prohibitions seem to be based on a simple statement about God's nature as Israel had experienced him in the course of their history. There is some evidence to suggest that in giving the commandments this precise form, the Old Testament writers may have had in mind the kind of covenant treaties that small struggling nations often made with more powerful states, in exchange for protection and security (see *The Old Testament Story*, page 47). Such covenant agreements would be reaffirmed at regular intervals. Alt believed that 'apodictic' laws of this kind formed the centre of

Exodus 20:1–17; Deuteronomy 5:6–22

Deuteronomy 31:9–13

Israel's renewal of her faith in God every seven years at the Festival of Shelters, or Tabernacles. It was this form of absolute law that was most characteristic of the Old Testament, for it was nothing less than an explanation of the everyday ramifications of Israel's covenant faith.

But there are difficulties with this view:

● Casuistic law is a distinctive literary form. But this so-called 'apodictic' law is not strictly a literary form at all. These absolute laws are expressed in a variety of literary formulations.

● Alt believed that these absolute rules were unique to Israel. But we now know that similar terminology could also be used in legal contexts elsewhere, especially among the Hittites, but also in Egypt and Babylon. It was not always the same actions that were prohibited there, of course, but the form itself was certainly found outside the Old Testament faith.

● There is no real evidence that these 'apodictic' laws either originated in or were regularly repeated at the great religious festivals in Israel.

● These statements are not really 'law' in the technical sense at all. They are a more general listing of accepted standards of behaviour, and in this respect the 'apodictic' law is not all that different from the teaching of the wisdom books. It is at least arguable that they could be based on Israel's understanding of the 'natural law' revealed in the work of creation, and not on the covenant at Mt Sinai.

Old Testament Law Codes

The books of *Torah* in the Old Testament, like all modern collections of law (and many other parts of the Old Testament), are an anthology of laws relating to different situations and different periods during the whole span of the Old Testament story. They are not meant to be read from start to finish as a consistent account of Israel's legal system. All scholars would agree that within the books of the Law there are at least four quite different collections of material. The precise way in which we relate these separate law codes to one another will be determined by our view of how the first five books of the Old Testament came to be written. This is extensively discussed in *The Old Testament Story*, pages 152-56, and our discussion here takes account of what is said there.

The Ten Commandments

Exodus 20:1–17

Most people who know anything at all about the Bible will recognize this collection of moral rules as a basic part of the Old Testament's view of human behaviour. Its principles have been enshrined in many national law codes since Old Testament days, and in many respects form a charter of fundamental human rights. It was obviously intended to be learned by heart, and often repeated. The fact that there are ten commandments is certainly not accidental, but is a learning device so that they could be counted off on the fingers of both hands as they were repeated. This was a popular way of remembering things.

There are other groups of laws which may originally have been

Exodus 34:12–26; Leviticus 20:2–16;
18:6–18

Psalm 15:2–5

organized in the same way, though they are mostly concerned with the conduct of organized worship. The book of Psalms contains at least one such list of ten things that summarize good behaviour. This is the main subject of the Ten Commandments themselves. They are not technically law, for they contain no mention of penalties for those who break them. Rather, they are a kind of policy statement – a bill of rights – showing how relationships between God and his people were to be viewed within the Old Testament faith community. It is widely agreed by scholars that this list must have originated at a very early period in the Old Testament story, quite possibly with Moses himself.

The book of the covenant

Exodus 20:22 — 23:33

Many parts of the book of the covenant are similar to other ancient law codes, especially the codes of Ur-Nammu of Ur (2050 BC) and of Hammurabi, king of Babylon (1700 BC). Though there are many differences of detail between the Book of the Covenant and these other laws, their general outlook is the same and simply reflects widespread customs in the ancient Middle East. So this is much more like a code of law in our modern sense. It is widely believed to be very ancient, going back to the time of Israel's earliest leaders, Moses and Joshua. The essential concern of these laws is with the life of the community. They are mostly a 'casuistic' type of legislation, though there are also some rules relating to the conduct of organized worship.

Crimes of violence are punished in nearly all societies.

Deuteronomy

The word 'Deuteronomy' means 'a second law'. Here we find an amplification and application of earlier law codes, showing how they could apply to the changing circumstances of Israel's national life. As such, it is obviously based on ancient materials. Some scholars believe that it found its present form as a liturgy for a covenant renewal festival at which the worshippers in ancient Israel would regularly 'relive' the events of their national past, and commit themselves afresh to their God Yahweh. Much of the book certainly reads like sermons, preached as a prelude to the presentation of the actual Law itself, and followed by the people's commitment to it. The book of Deuteronomy was a major influence in the reform of temple worship carried out by King Josiah of Judah, though its actual origins were certainly earlier than his day. See further on this *The Old Testament Story*, pages 131-32.

Deuteronomy 5 — 11
Deuteronomy 12 — 26
Deuteronomy 27 — 28

2 Kings 22:3–20

Priestly laws

These are found in Exodus, Leviticus and Numbers. They include all the rest of the Old Testament laws, among which are large sections dealing with the tent of worship and its contents, and various regulations for the priests there. There are also detailed regulations for the conduct of worship, together with rules governing the preparation and eating of food as well as matters of domestic and personal hygiene. It was once believed that these rules concerning worship were relatively late developments in the Old Testament story, partly because the message of the sixth-century prophet Ezekiel contains some similar notions. But closer investigation has shown that many of the practices referred to here are very similar to practices known elsewhere in the ancient world at a much earlier date.

Exodus 25 — 30
Exodus 35 — 40
Leviticus 1 — 10

Leviticus 11 — 16

Ezekiel 40 — 48

Leviticus 17 — 26

One section of the book of Leviticus is often thought to be another separate law code — the 'Holiness Code'. There are several reasons for this:

● These chapters begin with rules about organized worship, but then make no reference at all to the very full legislation on the matter found in the preceding chapters.

Leviticus 26:46

● The statement that 'All these are the laws and commands that the Lord gave to Moses on Mt Sinai for the people of Israel' seems to be a formal ending, which does not relate to what follows in the next chapter.

● The theme of 'holiness' runs everywhere through these chapters but is not a prominent theme at all in the rest of Leviticus.

Putting the Law into Practice

Life in the ancient world was totally different from life today, and most modern readers find the laws of the Old Testament dull and tedious. But they can still give us a number of insights into important aspects of the Old Testament faith. There seem to be so many collections of laws that it comes as a surprise to discover they are far from comprehensive. Many situations are not mentioned at all. Other ancient law codes were the same, perhaps because the laws that were written down were only intended as samples of how justice should be administered. Or it could be that the written laws were to give guidance in cases of particular difficulty, and alongside them other more straightforward procedures were simply taken for granted.

There are many ways of classifying laws. For our purpose here it will be helpful to consider how they related in general terms to the life of Israelite society. One area of life controlled by the Law was what we would call religion. Many Old Testament laws are 'cultic laws', describing how worship is to be conducted. This is considered more fully in the next chapter – though we must never forget that religion and everday behaviour can not easily be separated in the Old Testament. But in addition to that, we can trace four other types of law in the Old Testament codes.

Criminal law

Covenant treaties, like this one found in Alalah in modern Syria, were common in Old Testament times, and the 'covenant' is a basic Old Testament theme. Some believe the Ten Commandments take their form from the typical covenant treaty.

Exodus 22:20; Leviticus 20:1–5;
Deuteronomy 13:1–18
Leviticus 24:10–16
Exodus 22:18; Leviticus 20:27
Leviticus 21:9
Exodus 31:14–15

Every society has certain actions that are so thoroughly and universally disapproved of that the community itself feels it necessary to punish those who do them. Civil law deals with arguments between individuals, about which there can be room for different judgments. But criminal law concerns principles of right and wrong that are taken as self-evident. This does not mean that the criminal law of one nation will always be the same as the criminal law of another. Indeed, there are often striking differences. Even today, activities that are branded as criminal in one state may well be regarded as fundamental human rights in another. So by examining those actions which a particular state regards as criminal, we can soon understand the basic attitudes and fundamental values of its people.

As far as we can see, the only penalty actually exacted by the state in ancient Israel was the death penalty. Fines were unknown, and though a person could be put under arrest while his case was decided, imprisonment as such was not introduced until after the exile in Babylon. Monetary sanctions could be imposed, but they were regarded as restitution by the wrongdoer to the victim – and therefore came within the jurisdiction of the civil law. Even crimes such as personal assault or theft were dealt with in this way.

It is probably significant that every crime punishable by death was related in some way or another to the Ten Commandments. This is why Dr Anthony Phillips describes these Commandments as 'Ancient Israel's Criminal Law'. We have noticed that the Ten Commandments are not strictly 'law' at all in the technical sense. But this description is still a useful one, for all those actions punishable by the community as a whole were closely related to Israel's understanding of her position as the people of God. To commit a crime was, quite simply, to deny the reality of the covenant faith. Such crimes included:

● **Offences against God** Examples of these offences are idolatry, blasphemy and magic – all of which in one way or another deny the very basis of the relationship between God and his people. Other offences, such as the prostitution of a priest's daughter or not keeping the sabbath day might seem less serious to us. But the Old Testament Law views them in the same light because both

Exodus 31:16

priesthood and sabbath are 'a sign of the covenant'.

Exodus 21:12; Leviticus
24:17; Numbers 35:16–21
Numbers 35:22–29
Exodus 21:16; Deuteronomy 24:7

● **Offences against human life** Intentional murder was a particularly serious crime, though accidental killing was subject to other arrangements. No less serious was the case of a person who kidnaps another, intending to make him a slave. Human liberty as well as human life is of great value. Many scholars believe that the eighth commandment refers not to stealing in general but to kidnapping. The theme of personal freedom is certainly important in other sections of Old Testament Law.

Exodus 20:15; Deuteronomy 5:19

● **Offences against the family** If unnatural termination of life is a criminal offence, so is interference with the natural context in which life is created: the sexual relationship between husband and wife. Other kinds of sexual relationship, whether incest, homosexuality, buggery, or even adultery are all regarded as serious criminal offences, along with disdain for parents.

Leviticus 20:10–16
Exodus 21:15, 17; Leviticus 20:9;
Deuteronomy 21:18–21

Civil law

Old Testament civil law has many similarities to other laws of the ancient world. It deals with everyday affairs such as the treatment of employees, violence of various sorts, and the duties of owners to protect third parties from injury caused by either animals or property. The Book of the Covenant consists entirely of this sort of law. It is instructive that in this law code God is usually referred to as 'Elohim', meaning 'God' in general, rather than by his personal

Boundary stones marked the limits of a person's land; this one comes from Babylon in the time of Nebuchadnezzar I. Some Old Testament laws were aimed at preventing the absorption of smallholdings into great estates.

name 'Yahweh'. This may well suggest that Israel simply took over this legal form from the general stock of commonly accepted norms without making too many detailed changes to it.

Punishment is generally understood as compensation for the wrong done, and many penalties are similar to those in other codes such as the laws of Hammurabi. But there are some differences. Bodily mutilation, for example, was quite a common punishment in the ancient world, but there is only one specific example of it in the

Deuteronomy 25:11–12

Old Testament. The Old Testament certainly states that punishments should be exacted 'life for life, eye for eye, tooth for tooth,

Exodus 21:23–24; Leviticus 24:19–20; Deuteronomy 19:21

hand for hand, foot for foot, burn for burn, wound for wound, bruise for bruise'. But this seems to be almost a symbolic statement, emphasizing that the punishment should always be in proportion to the wrong that has been suffered. In the ancient world, even this apparently ruthless retribution could be a means of limiting what would otherwise be excessive vengeance. In the light of Lamech's

Genesis 4:23

boast that 'I have killed a young man because he struck me', even a basic law of equal retribution would be an improvement! In the event, though the principle is stated in the Book of the Covenant, it is both preceded and followed there by laws which show that in general other forms than physical punishment could and should be preferred – generally financial compensation. The payment of compensation to the victim in place of physical punishment was probably quite a widespread practice.

Family law

The whole of Israelite society was family and clan based, and the importance of the family unit is reflected in many Old Testament laws. Relationships between family members had a far-reaching effect on the overall shape of Israelite society.

A stable relationship between husband and wife was basic to the Old Testament view of family life. Marriage itself was generally of one man to one woman (monogamy), though kings and other leading figures often seem to have had more than one wife (polygamy) – and this practice is never actually banned anywhere in the Old Testament. Marriages were generally arranged by parents, though

1 Samuel 18:20

love marriages are not altogether unknown. But alongside his legal wife, a man could also have any number of 'concubines'. These were slave wives, and had a correspondingly lower status than the main wife. Divorce was taken for granted, though in practice it could often leave a woman destitute and was probably not very frequent for that reason.

But all these matters were entirely a family affair. The Law was not involved at all, except that the civil law contains a number of guidelines relating to circumstances that might arise with a breakdown of normal relationships, and the criminal law of course

Exodus 21:7–11; Deuteronomy 21:10–14
Deuteronomy 24:1–4

forbids adultery. Detailed regulations are given for the proper treatment of concubines. Guidance is also given on what should happen after a divorce.

Wilful disregard for parents was in certain circumstances dealt with by the criminal law, but usually the authority of the father or

Genesis 38:24
Deuteronomy 21:18–21

2 Samuel 14:4–11

Leviticus 25:47–49

patriarch of the family was absolute. In the earliest period, a father could even condemn members of his family to death. Later legislation provided for such cases to be referred to the village elders, and some passages suggest there was an ultimate right of appeal to the king.

On the positive side, members of a family also had obligations to each other. If one member was forced to sell himself into slavery to pay off a debt, then it was the duty of one of his close relatives to buy him back – circumstances which are well illustrated in the story of Ruth. Family life in Old Testament times could have definite advantages; but it also carried with it awesome responsibilities.

Social law

The Canaanite city-states which preceded the emergence of Israel as a nation were essentially feudal societies, with a powerful and wealthy ruling class. This was in strong contrast to the tribal structure we find in the Old Testament, which ensured that Israelite society was not dominated by a powerful hierarchy. Instead, it was a self-consciously egalitarian society in which all citizens enjoyed the same fundamental rights and privileges.

1 Samuel 8
Deuteronomy 17:14–20

The conflict between these two models of society runs deep in the Old Testament. In the earliest Israelite settlements, local elders were the leaders of their own communities. As things developed authority became more centralized until the need for a king was obvious. The Old Testament story documents the way the kingship was strenuously resisted. Even then, the power of the king was stringently regulated by the Law. When the great kingdom split in two after Solomon's death, it was largely the result of tensions between the Canaanite, bureaucratic ideal and the Israelite ideal in which every individual was equal – his freedom restricted only by the mutual obligations imposed by the family group.

1 Samuel 8:11–17

Leviticus 25:23

In practical terms, the central issue was the possession of land. In the Canaanite city-states all land was ultimately owned by the king. But in Israel, all land ultimately belonged to God himself. It was given in trust to the family group as something that could be neither bought nor sold, but must be handed on from one generation to the next. In this way Israel hoped to avoid the emergence of a land-owning class, and to preserve the relative equality of people. Those who tried to amass land for themselves were tirelessly condemned by the prophets. Even the king himself was not exempt. This is why apparently tedious lists of people and land play an important part in the Old Testament.

Isaiah 5:8
Micah 2:1–2
1 Kings 21

Numbers 26; 34; Joshua 13 — 19

Deuteronomy 19:14

Many laws set out to preserve the freedom of the individual to live unmolested on the land which God had given to the family. The Law banned actions such as moving boundary stones, and many other prohibitions relating to loans and debts also find their real significance in this context. Charging interest on loans was forbidden. But what often happened was that a person would give either clothes or property as security for a loan. Then, if the loan could not be repaid, the borrower soon became virtually a slave of the lender – and though technically living on his family land, he was reduced to a

Exodus 22:25; Leviticus 25:35–38;
Deuteronomy 23:19–20

state of destitution. This is why the Law tried to regulate what could be used as securities for loans. It also provided for debts to be written off every seven years (the sabbatical year), or every fifty years (the Jubilee).

Exodus 22:26–27; Deuteronomy 24:6
Deuteronomy 15:1–11
Leviticus 25:8–17

The Old Testament social ethic shows great concern for many disadvantaged groups – foreigners, the poor, the oppressed, widows, orphans, and even personal enemies. This emphasis has led some recent scholars to think of early Israel as a proletarian protest movement against the elitist structures of Canaanite power. There is a good deal to be said in favour of this view of Israel's social perception. But we must not exaggerate its uniqueness. Concern for despised people was not an exclusively Old Testament interest. In the laws of Ur-Nammu we read the following list of the king's achievements:

Exodus 22:21–27; 23:1–9

> The orphan was not delivered up to the rich man, the widow was not delivered up to the mighty man, the man of one shekel was not delivered up to the man of one mina.

The Old Testament is most distinctive in its treatment of slaves, who were clearly regarded as persons in their own right. Not only could they expect to be set free, but they also had rights even if they ran away from their master. The master must give his slaves a regular day off, and he must recognize the limits to his power over a slave's life. The master who injures his slave can be forced to compensate him by giving the slave his freedom.

Exodus 21:1–6
Deuteronomy 23:15–16
Exodus 23:12; Deuteronomy 5:12–15

Exodus 21:26–27

If a master kills his own slave, that is a particularly serious offence, and is to be avenged by the community acting on behalf of the slave, presumably because he has no family of his own to defend him. Some scholars believe that the death penalty was prescribed for this. If so, such concern for the welfare of slaves would be absolutely without parallel in the ancient world. It would also suggest that the killing of a slave represented a spiritual as well as a social challenge to the community. The religious background to the slavery laws is certainly made clear in at least one law code, where special treatment of slaves is justified by the statement that 'you were slaves in Egypt and the Lord your God set you free; that is why I am now giving you this command'. The distinctive nature of Israelite society emerged not out of purely humanitarian motives: it was part and parcel of Israel's experience of their God in the formative events of the nation's history.

Exodus 21:20

Deuteronomy 15:15

Explaining God's will

The impact of Israel's history can be seen most clearly in the sort of society envisaged by the Old Testament. In one way or another, all the most distinctive features of Old Testament morality have been determined by Israel's encounter with God on the stage of human history. The great events which helped formulate Israel's understanding of God's character also gave a special insight into what God required of his people. Events such as the escape from Egypt and the entry into the promised land had their effect on God's people and

These slaves in Assyria at the time of Sennacherib were far worse off than slaves in Israel, where the laws protected them at many points.

their behaviour. In the Old Testament, correct behaviour, like so many other things, was based on history.

But how can the facts of history tell you how to behave? As we read the messages of the great prophets and explore the teaching of the books of Law, the answer to the question soon emerges. For the Old Testament ethic is not only historical: it also has other characteristics that can be identified by an appreciation of God's involvement in the lives of his people.

The Old Testament ethic is theological

It is 'theological' in the strict meaning of that word, for the Old Testament code of behaviour always refers us back to God himself. Correct human behaviour is closely related to the kind of God who had revealed himself in the events of Israel's history. It is, of course, always true that the kind of god people believe in affects the way they behave. Many people today look on religion as a kind of insurance policy for the future. They think of God as more concerned with the next world than with this, and as a result their lifestyle now is often motivated by pure self-interest. But others who understand God as a person to be known and loved here and now will have quite a different attitude to contemporary social realities, and their lifestyle will reflect their concern. The Old Testament stresses that God is a personal and active being who can be known both by individuals and societies in the context of their everyday experience of life. It takes these characteristics of God and applies them directly to the life of his people. In the Old Testament human goodness finds its authority, example and inspiration in the person of God himself. Nowhere is this summed up more eloquently than in the book of Leviticus: 'Be holy, because I, the Lord your God, am holy.' God's

Leviticus 19:2

people are to behave like God behaves. The German scholar Emil Brunner summed it up concisely when he described Old Testament morality as 'the science of human conduct as it is determined by divine conduct'.

The Old Testament ethic is dynamic

How does God express his own personality? We have already seen that the Old Testament never tries to analyze or define God in an abstract way. He is never described 'metaphysically', by asking what he is made of. He is always described 'functionally', by reference to what he does. Obviously, the two are closely related, because the way people are will be reflected in the way they work. But the Old Testament God is not just a 'God who is' – he is a 'God who acts'. He is a dynamic God rather than a static one.

So what can we learn about human behaviour by looking at the characteristic actions of God himself? Three terms are often used in the Old Testament to describe God's moral disposition:

● **Justice** This might seem a very abstract idea to us. 'Justice' is the kind of thing that lawyers and judges argue about in law courts. In the Old Testament, 'justice' includes this concern for fair play. But more characteristically justice is not something to talk about – it is something to be done. The leaders of early Israel were not 'judges' in the modern legal sense: they were leaders of their people who saw something wrong, and did something to put it right. Indeed, the Hebrew word that is normally translated 'justice' in our English Old Testament really has a much wider meaning. It refers to everything that a ruler might do to ensure that his people would enjoy a stable

One of the great formative experiences of Israel's history was their entry into the promised land, seen here from across the north end of the Dead Sea. The people were called to remember that their land was held in trust from God.

and satisfying way of life. God, therefore, is like a 'just' ruler: he improves the quality of life for his people.

● Mercy When this word is used to describe God, it is emphasizing that he deals with people in a loving and personal way. God's justice is not determined by the stringent requirements of some legal system: it always operates in a context of personal love and trust. The entire Old Testament story shows how, against all expectations, God has initiated a relationship with people who by nature are weak and often morally and spiritually powerless. God never abandons them. Instead, he stands alongside them to help in their weakness, and will never reject them despite all their inadequacy and imperfection. 'How can I give you up, Israel? How can I abandon you? ... My heart will not let me do it! My love for you is too strong ... For I am God and not man. I, the Holy One, am with you. I will not come to you in anger.'

● Truth This is also something that we tend to think of in abstract terms. But in the Old Testament, 'truth' is more often a characteristic of people. When the disguised Joseph put his brothers in prison, he did so to find out 'whether there is truth in you' – in other words, whether they could be trusted or not. In the world of the Old Testament the gods were notoriously unreliable. They did whatever they wished, and all too often their human worshippers had to pay the price. But the God of the Old Testament is quite different. He is wholly trustworthy, and it is upon God's faithfulness that his people can stake their own destiny: 'I have complete confidence, O God! ... Your constant love reaches above the heavens; your faithfulness touches the skies.'

In these three respects, God's people are called upon to imitate him. Following his example is not just a matter of believing certain things about God: it is supremely a matter of behaving as he behaves.

The Old Testament ethic is social

In what context is God's will most truly done? Is God concerned with the moral goodness of individuals – or with the shape of society? Inevitably, these two concerns are not mutually exclusive. Individual people are called upon to respond for themselves to the will of God. When Isaiah was confronted with the moral grandeur of God in the temple, he confessed to his own shortcomings and became intensely aware of his own personal inadequacy to do the work to which God was calling him. The story of Abraham pleading for the deliverance of two evil cities makes a similar point: that God cares about the behaviour of individuals. Yet throughout the Old Testament, there is also a major emphasis on the whole of God's people. God's will is to be shown not just in pious individuals, but in the structures of national life.

We have already seen this strong emphasis on social justice in both wisdom books and law codes, and it was born out of the formative events of Israel's history. On a social level, the exodus had demonstrated God's concern for those who were unjustly oppressed by the forces of imperialism. The God of the Bible was not like the paternalistic God of the cotton growers of the American south, who

Deuteronomy 32:4; Isaiah 5:16; 61:8

Hosea 11:8–9

Genesis 42:16

Psalm 108:1–4

Isaiah 6:5

Genesis 18:16–33

The Israelites were instructed to teach each generation the laws God had given.

in the nineteenth century used to encourage their black slaves by telling them that life would be better in heaven. Yahweh saw that things were bad in Egypt – and stepped in to change the situation. This is why the ideal Old Testament society always had a special place for the dispossessed, the oppressed and the disadvantaged. Moreover, the very fabric of society should reflect this concern. The prophets loved to remind their people that in Israel all men and women must be equal. They had all started out as equals – they were all slaves – and therefore economic and social exploitation of one class by another was not only deplorable: it was a fundamental denial of the very heart of the Old Testament faith.

The Old Testament ethic is personal

This brings us to the crux of the whole matter. Behaviour in the Old Testament is always seen in the context of the covenant that Israel had entered into with God. God was deeply involved in every aspect of the life of this world. He was not aloof from the human predicament. And his involvement was expressed in the notion of the covenant. For as Israel looked back to the foundation events of their national life, they saw the events of the exodus and what followed as the culmination of God's purpose for his people. In the memory of that momentous event, Israel found the meaning of their national life. As the freed slaves had stood before Mt Sinai they had been reminded of God's great and loving actions on their behalf. In return they were called upon to fulfil his commands and to be loyal to him. Israelite society was based on this mutual relationship of love and responsibility. As Israel met for worship in the annual cycle of the great religious festivals, each generation was able to commit itself afresh to this personal relationship between God and his people. This was where life found its deepest meaning. God had called his people in love when they were neither expecting nor deserving it – and succeeding generations would respond to that love by following the example of God himself.

When the Old Testament demands justice, mercy and truth in human relationships, it does not appeal to some abstract notion of morality. Instead, it goes back to the roots of the covenant faith, in the justice, mercy and truth of God himself. When the prophets call for righteousness in society, they look back to the actions of God himself in caring for outcasts and strangers. And it is no surprise that one of the most eloquent statements of God's will – the Ten Commandments – begins not with a command, but with a statement: 'I am the Lord your God who brought you out of Egypt, where you were slaves.' Right behaviour should stem naturally from the response of a grateful people to what God has done for them. Morality and theology are inextricably interwoven with each other – for it is within the context of a personal relationship between God and his people that the ethical principles of the Old Testament can most fully be understood.

Exodus 20:2

The administration of justice

We have examined the content of the Old Testament law codes in some detail. But how were these laws put into practice? What sort of legal structures existed in ancient Israel?

The answer to that question is quite complex, for Israelite society underwent a number of profound changes in the course of the events documented in the Old Testament. The life of the tribes in the days of the judges was socially and politically quite different from life in the kingdom of David and Solomon. Things changed again after their kingdom divided, and then following the demise of the northern kingdom of Israel. Changing circumstances inevitably led to changes in national institutions, and the administration of law varied from one century to another in the course of the Old Testament story.

But a number of individuals are mentioned in relation to the administration of justice, and consideration of their functions will give us an insight into some aspects of this complex subject.

The elders

Israelite society was always regarded as an extended family group. The head of each family had jurisdiction over his own relatives and household. The town or village elders were just the leading members of the various families. The Deuteronomic code mentions them quite specifically as acting as a regular court where disputes about the Law could be settled (Deuteronomy 19:12; 21:1–9,19–21; 22:13–21; 25:5–10). All the evidence suggests that this was the main law court throughout the entire history of Israel. The elders would meet at the gates of the town, which was a regular meeting place for serious discussion of the affairs of the community (Genesis 23:10–18; Job 29:7–10).

There was no official prosecutor, and the complainant would present the case against the accused in person. Some Old Testament passages suggest there would be an official 'defender' of the accused person (Psalm 109:31). Both prosecution and defence would call witnesses and produce material evidence (Exodus 22:13; Deuteronomy 22:13–17). Accusations and evidence would normally be presented verbally, though written statements could also be accepted (Job 31:35–36). The elders

would be seated during the trial, rising to pronounce their verdict. If a penalty was involved, then the elders would impose it and would usually carry it out on the spot (Deuteronomy 22:13–21).

The whole of this procedure reflects the view that most cases were essentially civil disputes between citizens. The job of the town elders was to adjudicate between them, and thereby see that justice was done. The story of the book of Ruth is a good illustration of how it worked in practice (Ruth 4:1–12).

The corruption of such local courts is a major theme in the prophets (Amos 5:10–15). It was all too easy for local elders to be swayed by their own prejudices, or even to accede to the wishes of a king who wanted to act unconstitutionally. The story of Naboth's trial and subsequent execution is a striking illustration of how the whole system could be abused by the powerful for their own advantage (1 Kings 21:1–16). Though false witnesses could be liable to severe penalties (Deuteronomy 19:15–20), this does not seem to have deterred perjury, and there is plenty of evidence to show that justice at the city gate was sometimes rough and ready.

The judges

As well as the courts of elders, the Old Testament also mentions professional judges (Deuteronomy 16:18–20; 19:16–18). The laws of Deuteronomy seem to envisage a system of local judges, with a final court of appeal in Jerusalem itself (Deuteronomy 17:8–13).

Albrecht Alt believed that the professional judge was important even in the earliest days of Israelite society. He equated them with the 'minor judges' (Judges 10:1–5; 12:8–15), and suggested that the law they administered was the casuistic law contained in the Book of the Covenant. Martin Noth incorporated this insight into his theory that early Israel was organized into a tribal amphictyony, and these 'minor judges' thereby became the guardians of the covenant theology which held the various tribes together. This view is further explained in *The Old Testament Story*, pages 64–66. But the main difficulty is that neither Alt nor Noth was ever able to produce any really compelling evidence to support it.

Others have argued that professional judges were a later development, perhaps originating in the southern Kingdom of Judah with the political and religious reforms of Jehoshaphat (875–851 BC) (2 Chronicles 19:4–11). They believe that the king always had

an important part to play in both establishing and maintaining the Law, and that when Jehoshaphat set up a legal system of professional judges he was merely formalizing a state of affairs that had existed for a long time.

The king

The king certainly had a role in the legal affairs of his people. All the ancient Middle Eastern law codes known to us are associated with kings, though quite often their function was limited to classifying customary procedures rather than actually originating the Law. Since the laws of a state are a vital part of its self-understanding, it was vital for the king to be involved in this way if his own position was to be maintained. But the Old Testament gives no real indication that the kings of either Israel or Judah operated in this way. Josiah perhaps came closest to publishing a law (2 Kings 23:1–3). But the story makes it clear that he was acting as an intermediary in a covenant renewal ceremony between God and the people, in much the same way as Moses (Exodus 24:3–8) and Joshua (Joshua 24:1–28) had done earlier, and as Ezra was to do later (Nehemiah 8:1–12). When the Old Testament explains the function of the king, there is no mention of law-giving, and he is himself firmly stated to be subject to the law of the covenant (1 Samuel 8:10–18; Deuteronomy 17:14–20).

Some scholars suggest this reflects the ideals of Old Testament kingship, rather than what actually happened in practice. But incidents in which the king overturns the normal course of justice always seem to be the exception rather than the rule in the Old Testament story. There is no substantial evidence that the king was in control of the legal process unless we are prepared to set aside almost the whole of the Deuteronomistic History as worthless and unreliable.

This need not mean that kings never issued law codes as part of their activity. Josiah was certainly involved in re-establishing the laws of Deuteronomy (see *The Old Testament Story*, pages 130–32). There is also good reason to think that the Book of the Covenant may have been collated and issued in the time of David and Solomon as a kind of constitution for their kingdom. But this did not make it 'state law', because it ultimately rested on a religious understanding of the life of the nation. It could just as easily be argued that when kings became

The laws of Israel covered every aspect of daily life. But how were they to be applied and enforced in practice?

involved in promoting the Law they were acting in a religious capacity rather than as purely political leaders.

There is also evidence that kings had a judicial function. The kingship itself apparently originated within the general framework of family and tribal life (1 Samuel 8:4–5). In that context the king would automatically be one of the 'elders' of the extended family of Israel. As such he would have a part to play in the administration of the law, probably acting as a final court of appeal (2 Samuel 12:1–6; 14:1–11; 1 Kings 3:16–28; 7:7).

The priests

Deuteronomy makes a close connexion between judges and priests, when it provides for a court of appeal in Jerusalem staffed by both priests and judges apparently operating on a rota basis (Deuteronomy 17:8–12). Priests and judges are found together elsewhere in the Old Testament (Deuteronomy 19:17; 2 Chronicles 19:8–11). In other ancient Middle Eastern states priests often had judicial functions. In Israel, the close connexion between Law and the covenant religion

made it inevitable that priests should be involved in interpreting and applying the Law.

No doubt this priestly function went back to a very early period of Old Testament history. Whatever may be the truth about the 'minor judges', there can be little doubt that like the 'major' judges they had a religious as well as a political and social function. Samuel, who appears as their successor, was essentially a priest operating from the shrines of Bethel, Gilgal and Mizpah. But his typical activities at these centres of worship were what we could call judicial (1 Samuel 7:16).

The precise judicial function of the priest is unclear from the Old Testament. Priests would certainly pronounce on religious affairs (Leviticus 10:10; 13:1–14:57). There are also hints that they could operate in a wider legal context (Leviticus 10:10–11; Deuteronomy 21:5; Ezekiel 44:24), though apart from the stories of Samuel there is no evidence of them ever doing so. Their more usual function would be as guardians of the final court of appeal: God himself. The Law allowed that in cases where a normal court could reach no verdict, God should be called in as the final judge. His will was discerned either by a procedure of judicial oaths (Exodus 22:6–13) or by drawing lots – something probably associated with the manipulation of urim and thummim (sacred stones or dice) by the priests (Joshua 7:1–19; 1 Samuel 14:41–43).

Individuals and the community

The Old Testament faith lays great emphasis on groups: the family, the clan, the tribe, and ultimately the nation, are all of fundamental importance both religiously and morally. The covenant itself is a relationship between God and the whole people of Israel, and salvation and judgment are both corporate experiences.

The processes of justice also take account of this corporate solidarity. When Achan stole some goods from the Canaanite city of Jericho, his entire family and all their goods shared in his punishment (Joshua 7:1–26). Some passages seem to elevate this to a general principle, that children will always be punished for the wrongs of their parents (Exodus 20:5; Deuteronomy 5:9). As a matter of common experience, it is true that any generation inevitably shares the legacy of the past. But the Old Testament makes a very clear connexion between past and present, the individual and the community. The prophets also emphasize corporate responsibility, pronouncing judgment on the whole nation because of the wrongs of some of its members (Amos 3:12–15; 5:16–24).

This emphasis was perhaps inevitable in a religion which was anchored to the events of history. If the exodus was to be relevant to later generations, then they had in some way to identify themselves with the experience of their ancestors. And when they went along to organize a worship at the shrines, they often did precisely that (Deuteronomy 26:5–10). This same connexion between the experience of an individual and the state of the community also comes out in some of the psalms. But the best example of it is in the passages referring to the suffering servant. For here, this one person both represents the community and fulfils its true destiny in his own spiritual experience (Isaiah 42:1–4; 49:1–6; 50:4–9; 52:13–53:12).

This way of thinking has often been described as 'corporate personality', and it has been assumed that the Old Testament has a unique way of looking at people and their relationships. On this view, the idea of personal responsibility only came into the Old Testament at a relatively late stage, when the group was in danger of disappearing altogether as an identifiable national entity. Jeremiah (31:29–30) and Ezekiel (18:4, 20) certainly emphasize that each person is responsible to God. But they do not really contradict the earlier Old Testament position. In their day, the people were blaming their problems onto past generations. In response to that Jeremiah and Ezekiel both emphasized that it was not that simple, for each individual must accept some share of responsibility for the state of society as a whole. In any case, there is plenty of evidence that individuals were believed to have moral and spiritual responsibility long before their time:

● Many individuals in the earlier parts of the Old Testament story are praised for their own personal response and commitment to God. Enoch (Genesis 5:21–24), Noah (Genesis 6:9–12) and Hannah (1 Samuel 1:9–2:11) – as well as the prophets – are all specifically described in terms of their own personal spiritual experience.

● Individuals are also condemned and judged for their own wrongdoing. When David committed adultery with Bathsheba, he himself suffered the penalty (2 Samuel 12:1–23). And when

Opposite
The memorial to the 'Unknown Soldier' in Washington, United States, is a modern counterpart to the sense of national togetherness felt by the people of Israel.

Jezebel met her death beneath the ramparts of Jezreel, that was considered a fair punishment for her malicious judicial murder of Naboth (2 Kings 9:30–37). Moreover, the law codes are full of instructions about how individuals are to be dealt with in the light of their own behaviour. The case of Achan, whose entire family was punished for his theft, is in fact exceptional. It was almost certainly considered to be a specifically religious crime – and for that reason was punishable under different rules.

● Amos seems to have condemned the whole nation without regard for personal responsibility, though he may have expected some to repent and avoid judgment (Amos 5:4–7,14–15). But other prophets clearly distinguished between the majority of the people who had broken the covenant and a small group who had not and who for that reason would escape punishment (Isaiah 10:20–22; Micah 5:7–8; Zephaniah 2:3; 3:11–13).

The idea of corporate solidarity is both less precise and less extensive than has often been thought. But it is also less distinctive than has sometimes been suggested. Many modern states have a parallel in their memorials to an 'unknown warrior'. This is a soldier who has been buried in a public place to be a lasting reminder of thousands of others like him, who died in battle and were buried in unmarked graves where they fell. When people pay their respects at such national monuments, they are not primarily honouring the soldier who happens to be interred there. Through him, they are honouring the memory of all those whom he represents. The analogy is not exact, for people in ancient Israel obviously felt this strong sense of solidarity at many other levels of everyday life. But a person's place in the nation never encompassed everything, and there was always a belief that people were morally and spiritually responsible to God as individuals.

5 Worshipping God

Worshipping a holy God

IN THE Old Testament, the need for worship is related to the fact that God is 'holy'. Today, the word 'holy' often has a rather vague meaning, sometimes indicating little more than 'religious'. But when the Old Testament describes Yahweh as 'holy' it is saying some very specific things about God and his relationships with people.

God is infinite

In the Old Testament story, God made himself known to his people in the events of their history and of their own everyday life. Because of this, we can understand a good deal about his nature and personality. But this never meant that ordinary people could know everything about God. When Job was trying to make sense out of his own frustrating life, he was forced to admit that in the last analysis there are hidden depths to God's workings that defy human understanding. Though God had revealed himself so clearly in events such as the exodus, there were still other aspects of his existence that were deeply mysterious. Nor was Job the only one to feel this way. Both poets and prophets knew that God was different from people. In chapter two we saw how God's apparent 'hiddenness' was a major part of Israel's experience on both a personal and a national level.

Job 30:1–31

Psalm 139:6
Isaiah 40:13–14

This feeling of perplexity and wonder in the face of an awe-inspiring divine presence is, of course, common to religious people the world over. So is the use of the word 'holy' to describe the difference between God and people. The literal meaning of the Hebrew word translated 'holy' is not certain, though many scholars think it is related to a word that means 'to divide'. When people describe the gods they worship as 'holy', they often think of the universe being divided into two quite different modes of existence. There is the place where God is – and people, things and events connected with it can be called 'holy'. Then there is also the world where we are – and that is 'profane' or 'common'. In this context, the words 'holy' and 'profane' do not indicate moral judgments: they are simply terms used to convey the fact that God and people are not the same. The Old Testament shares this widely-held view with other nations of both the ancient and the modern world.

Leviticus 10:10

Within this frame of reference, one aim of worship is to enable these two domains to meet and relate to each other. Even apparently 'common' things can be made 'holy' – places, times, people and objects. But once they have been consecrated to God in this way, special care must be taken by 'common' people in dealing with them. 'Holiness' is often spoken of in the Old Testament as if it were a great power or force, emanating from the very person of God himself. It is not easy for modern people in a technological society to understand this idea. But a parallel might be found in our own respect for the contents of the core of a nuclear reactor. Though most of us do not understand its workings, we all know that at the centre of the process are materials radiating out invisible rays of power that, if not properly contained and controlled by those competent to deal with them, could be disastrous for us all.

The Old Testament often uses similar sorts of imagery to describe

God's holy presence. When God revealed his will to Moses at Mt Sinai, his awesome presence was something that ordinary people must avoid. The place became so saturated with the divine power ('holiness') that only specially equipped people could cope with it. Ordinary people such as Moses could readily be set aside and themselves made holy, but if they came into contact with such holiness before that the results could be catastrophic. The Philistines learned this to their cost when they tried to meddle with the Ark of the Covenant.

Exodus 19:9–25

1 Samuel 5:1 — 6:19

But even an Israelite could suffer the same fate when he as a 'common' person came into contact with the 'holiness' of the divine presence.

2 Samuel 6:1–8

God's majesty and power must be respected, and to call God 'holy' is one way of emphasizing that. Though God can be known in a direct and personal way by his people, he is still God, to be esteemed and treated with due reverence.

Exodus 15:11; Job 11:7–12; Psalm 139:6–12

God is good

Many religious people think of their gods only in terms of awe-inspiring power. But Israel's covenant faith led to a distinctive understanding of what it means to be holy. In the world of religions, the mysterious, numinous, all-powerful kind of holiness has often been advanced as an explanation for the irrational and capricious actions of the gods. But the events of Israel's history had shown that the God of the Old Testament was faithful and trustworthy, not

Throughout the Old Testament the call to worship is sounded. People are summoned to come together and be joyful before God.

fickle and unpredictable. In the light of that, God's holiness was a way of behaving, not just a state of being. To say that God is holy means that he is good. And since people are by nature the very opposite of what God is, to describe him as 'holy' is also a confession of human failure.

Isaiah 55:8

These two aspects of God's holiness – the numinous and the ethical – are brought together most clearly in the experience of the prophet Isaiah as he went to the temple to worship. By definition, what went on in the temple was holy in the numinous sense – for the temple was a holy place, set apart for God's own use, and only those who were ritually holy themselves could cope with it. As the prophet stood there with the other worshippers, he had an awe-inspiring experience of God's greatness and power. But in response to this revelation, he at once recognized that a state of ritual cleanness was not enough by itself to equip him for God's presence. God's majestic holiness and his moral goodness could not be separated from each other, and Isaiah instantly knew that he was unfit to encounter God because of his own sinfulness.

Isaiah 6:1–7

This recognition was one of the greatest insights of the Old Testament prophets. In the various Canaanite cults it was widely assumed that God's holiness had only a cultic, numinous dimension, and that people could be made fit to deal with God by means of appropriate rituals. The people of Israel were constantly tempted to think the same way. But the prophets declared that they were wrong. God was concerned with everyday behaviour, not just with ritual at the shrine. Personal and social sin were incompatible with true worship.

Amos 5:21–24; Micah 6:6–8

It was not only the prophets who saw sin as a barrier to fellowship with God. The law codes make the same connexion between morals and worship – indeed, words that worshippers used in the temple itself often reminded them of precisely the same fact: 'Who has the right to go up the Lord's hill? Who may enter his holy temple? Those who are pure in act and in thought ...'

Psalm 24:3–4

God is love

Isaiah 6:5

For Isaiah, the painful awareness of God's moral holiness was inextricably linked to his need for forgiveness. A way must be found by which the sinful prophet could be made fit for the presence of such a holy God. In numinous terms, a person could be made fit to deal with holiness by undergoing the required cultic procedures. But how could moral reformation be brought about? Like others both before and after him, Isaiah knew only too well that human effort could not improve things. If he was to be morally right with God, then God himself would have to do it. And so the means of Isaiah's spiritual reconciliation comes from God himself. A burning coal is brought from the altar. Through this symbolic act he is told 'your guilt is gone, and your sins are forgiven'.

Isaiah 6:7

The book of Isaiah frequently calls God 'the holy one' precisely because he forgives sin and brings salvation to the lives of his people. Yes, God is the Almighty, the Infinite. Yes, he is morally perfect. But he cares for sinful people. To say he is 'holy' not only defines his

Isaiah 43:14–15; 45:11–13

awesome power: it also implies his perfect love. God's holy presence condemns human sin – but it also provides the means whereby sin can be forgiven: 'I am the high and holy God, who lives for ever. I live in a high and holy place, but I also live with people who are humble and repentant, so that I can restore their confidence and hope.'

Isaiah 57:15

This is the background against which we must understand Old Testament worship. Sincere worship reflects the response of God's people to the revelation of God's nature – and the nature of God's holiness determines the character of the human response. Because God is almighty, true worship must always respect the barriers between the sacred and the secular, the holy and the profane. Because he is good, true worship must honestly face up to the reality of human sin. But because he is love, the repentant worshipper can always look for God's forgiveness and the promise of a renewed life. The precise way in which these themes are related to each other varies from one occasion of worship to another. But all worship begins from the recognition that God is holy and people are not. It is a celebration of the many ways in which they can be made fit for God's presence.

Places of worship

Modern Christian places of worship are simply buildings where large numbers of people can meet together. Their size, shape and location are often determined by social convenience rather than by any particularly religious considerations. In principle, a Christian place of worship could be built anywhere. Indeed, Christians can (and often do) meet for worship without special buildings – in schools, public halls, or even the open air.

But in ancient Israel things were quite different. A legitimate place of worship needed to be a recognizably 'holy' place – a spot at which God had revealed himself in a specific way, and which men and women could therefore assume was a place where the holiness of God's presence could safely meet the profane life of the world. When Moses encountered the burning bush in the desert, he recognized it as just such a place (Exodus 3:5–6). That particular spot never became a regular place of worship, presumably because of its distance from the main centres of population in later Israel. But later generations had many such places where they could worship God, because he had previously met there with the leaders of their nation. Inevitably, the most popular places of worship changed with the passage of time. As we read the Old Testament story we can trace a number of significant stages.

The tent of the Lord's presence

In the earliest days of Israel's history, the tribes who escaped from Egypt worshipped God in a special tent erected in the centre of their camp (Exodus 33:7 – 40:38). The Old Testament uses a variety of terms to describe this tent. It is often referred to as the tent of the Lord's presence, or 'tabernacle'. The practice of having such a place for worship is not unusual among nomadic tribes in the Middle East even today. God's presence in this sanctuary (his 'holiness') was symbolized by the cloud which covered it. The movement of this cloud provided the signal for the tribes to move on.

The Old Testament provides detailed instructions for the erection and use of this portable sanctuary. There is considerable debate among scholars as to the precise origin of these instructions, but the general picture they give is typical of many ancient places of worship. A central enclosure marked the most holy part of the tent (the holy of holies). It was surrounded by various other enclosures until the boundary of the shrine was reached. Beyond this were the tents of the priests and those of the people. Such an arrangement was found in every place of worship throughout the whole of the

Old Testament story. It was designed 'to separate what was holy from what was not' (Ezekiel 42:20), and to ensure that only those who were properly qualified would come into contact with the awesome holiness of God's presence at the very centre of the sanctuary.

The sacred tents of bedouin tribes would normally have an image of their god within the most holy place. But Israel never portrayed God as an idol. Instead, the holy of holies contained the Ark of the Covenant. There is a good deal of uncertainty about the precise significance of this Ark. In appearance it was a wooden box overlaid with gold and decorated with various religious symbols. Perhaps the people thought of it as an empty throne where the invisible Yahweh could sit enthroned in glory. It was certainly identified very closely with God's personal presence (Numbers 10:35–36; Joshua 4:5,13). In the period of the judges the various tribes were able to unite around this symbolic representation of God's presence in their midst (see *The Old Testament Story*, pages 46–47, 64–66).

We do not know for sure what happened to either the Ark or the tent of the Lord's presence. The Ark is mentioned a number of times after the desert period. It was present at the crossing of the River Jordan (Joshua 3:1–5:1). Later it was kept at Bethel (Judges 20:18–28), but was then captured from the sanctuary at Shiloh by the Philistines in the time of Samuel (1 Samuel 4:1–7:1). Still later, it was taken to Jerusalem by David (2 Samuel 6:1–23), where Solomon finally installed it in the temple he built (1 Kings 8:1–9). It may well have been used in religious festivals at Jerusalem (Psalm 24:7–10; 48:12–14;132:1–18), and it was probably either destroyed or taken away by the Babylonian Nebuchadnezzar when he overthrew Jerusalem in 586 BC. In any event, after the exile its place in the temple was probably occupied by a gold plate, and by New Testament times the holy of holies was completely empty (*Jewish wars V.v.5*).

The tent of the Lord's presence disappeared from sight even earlier than the Ark. Indeed, there are no certain references to it after the tribes had settled in the land of Canaan. Some passages seem to imply that it was at one stage erected at Shiloh (Joshua 18:1; 19:51; 1 Samuel 2:22). But if that was the case it cannot have lasted long, for by the time of Samuel Shiloh had a permanent building for worship (1 Samuel 1:7,9; 3:15). There is also a

reference to 'the tent of the Lord' at Gibeon in the time of Solomon (1 Chronicles 16:39), though the precise meaning of the phrase there is uncertain. David placed the Ark of the Covenant in a tent when he first took it to Jerusalem (2 Samuel 6:17, 7:2; 1 Kings 1:39). But although this was undoubtedly intended to recall the tent of the Lord's presence, there is no suggestion that it was this original tent that he erected.

Both Ark and tent played an important role in the development of the Old Testament faith. By their very nature they were a challenge to the widespread view that gods were restricted in power and influence to particular places and peoples. It was always a temptation for the settling tribes to imagine that God's power extended only over the desert – and as a result they found themselves tempted to worship the gods and goddesses of Canaan. Later on, in the time of Jeremiah, just before the final collapse of the kingdom of Judah, the people of Jerusalem were tempted to suppose that their city would never fall because God lived there – in the temple (Jeremiah 7:1–15). Both attitudes were understandable. But both were false, and when a later prophet declared that Israel's God was in reality the God of the whole world, he was articulating something that had been implicit in the Old Testament faith from a very early period (Isaiah 44:1–8).

Local sanctuaries

People always like to worship where they live, and the local sanctuaries in towns and villages throughout the land had an important part to play for most of the Old Testament period. Almost every settlement must have had its own place of worship. Not all of them would be buildings. A majority may have been little more than altars in the open air at which regular sacrifices could be offered. A great many such altars have been discovered by archaeologists throughout Palestine. Sometimes they were constructed from heaps of stones. At other times a natural feature of the landscape or a particularly striking rock would be used for the purpose.

The stories of the patriarchs show the earliest ancestors of Israel worshipping at a great number of such local sanctuaries right across the country – places such as Hebron (Genesis 13:18; 18:1–15), Beersheba (Genesis 26:23–26) and Mizpah (Genesis 31:43–55). These places were most likely Canaanite places of worship long before the Hebrew patriarchs arrived in the land, though the Old Testament generally points out that it was really the covenant God Yahweh whom they worshipped there. At other times the patriarchs are depicted establishing new centres of worship. When Jacob had an unusual dream in the open air, he recognized it as a holy place because God met him there. As a result, he called it 'Bethel', meaning 'the house of God'(Genesis 28:10–22). Later generations of Israelites regarded it as a particularly holy place (Judges 20:18–28; 1 Samuel 7:16; 10:3). After the collapse of Solomon's united kingdom, Bethel became one of the major sanctuaries of the northern kingdom of Israel (1 Kings 12:29–13:32; Amos 3:14; 4:4; 5:5–6; 7:10–13).

Local places of worship play an important part in the Old Testament story. The stories about Samuel associate him with the sanctuaries at Bethel, Gilgal, Mizpah, Ramah and Shiloh (1 Samuel 1:1–3:21, 7:16–17). The shrine at Shiloh seems to have been of sufficient importance to be

called a temple. After its destruction by the Philistines in about 1050 BC the centre of attention moved to other places, notably Gilgal and Mizpah, both of which are connected with significant stages in Saul's career as king (1 Samuel 11:14–15; 13:8–15; 10:17–27). Later, king Solomon was a regular visitor to a sanctuary at Gibeon. On one occasion there he had a dream in which he met God and was promised the gift of wisdom (1 Kings 3:4–15).

Gibeon is described as 'the most famour altar' of all (1 Kings 3:4). But that situation soon changed, when Solomon built his great temple in Jerusalem (1 Kings 5:1–6:37). After that, the local sanctuaries must have been put in the shade by the splendour of worship in the temple. The large staff of priests and other officials there made worship so much more impressive and exciting than what went on in smaller towns and villages – and it was not long before large crowds were making regular pilgrimages to Jerusalem. This was what Solomon had wanted – for political as well as religious reasons. But

During the Israelites' time as desert nomads, the central place in their camp was given to the 'tent of the Lord's presence' or 'tabernacle', with the Ark of the Covenant in its holy of holies. The altar for sacrifice stood on open ground outside the tent itself.

it meant that smaller shrines had to struggle to survive. Many local places of worship probably fell into disuse at this period. Many more tried to get the worshippers back by reviving Canaanite forms of worship that the Old Testament denounces as departures from the true covenant faith. Such worship was certainly widespread. Looking back at this time, Jeremiah could later comment that 'On every high hill and under every green tree you worshipped fertility gods'(Jeremiah 2:20). This complaint had particular relevance to the sanctuaries of the northern kingdom. But even in Judah every later attempt at religious reform involved the forcible closure of these local sanctuaries which had become centres of alien worship (2 Kings 18:1–8; 21:3; 23:1–20).

The temple

The temple in Jerusalem came to occupy a special place in the devotion of the people. Its unique position was celebrated in much of ancient Israel's best-loved poetry. It symbolized all the distinctive features of the Old Testament faith, uniting the political and the religious aspirations of the people, centred on the kings who ruled

from Jerusalem as the successors of David. Devotion to the temple could sometimes lead to misplaced nationalism.It did so in the days of Jeremiah when the inhabitants of Jerusalem were certain that nothing could happen to their city because the temple was there (Jeremiah 7:1–15). The prophets had to remind them that God's holy presence in the temple could bring judgment as well as salvation. It was possible to preserve the external appearance of true worship when in reality God's presence was no longer there (Ezekiel 10:1–22).

The Old Testament gives fairly detailed accounts of the building of the temple by Solomon (1 Kings 6:1–7:51; 2 Chronicles 2:17–5:1). But the details of the design are obscure, and when modern scholars have tried to reconstruct models of the temple they have produced a number of different proposals. It is clear that the general layout was similar to many other temples throughout the ancient Middle East (though no precisely identical temple has been found elsewhere). This general similarity is not surprising, as Solomon needed to import workers from Phoenicia to design and build it (1 Kings 5:1–12; 7:13–14) – presumably

Some details of Israelite worship echoed the cults of the surrounding peoples, though Israel's monotheism made the central thrust quite different. The pomegranate decorations (right) are Canaanite, and the cult stand (centre above) is Philistine. But the cherub and the shrine with pillars (model) are Israelite.

because Israel had no previous experience of a large-scale building project.

In general terms, the layout of the temple was similar to the design of the tent of the Lord's presence, with a central holy of holies surrounded by other spaces and enclosures. Indeed, some scholars believe that the Old Testament's descriptions of the temple and the tent are quite closely related to each other. The basic structure consisted of three rooms: an entrance hall, a main room and, at a slightly higher level, the holy of holies. Whereas the entrance hall and main room were rectangular, with the doors on the shorter sides, the holy of holies was a cube. As in the tent of the Lord's presence, the holy of holies contained the Ark of the Covenant – with two large golden cherubim suspended from the ceiling over the place where the Ark was kept.

Most of the worship, however, took place not in the holy of holies but in the other parts of the temple building and courtyards. The actual contents of these areas varied from time to time, and the religious symbols and altars used there were often as much an indication of the nation's political alliances as of its

spiritual commitment. When Ahaz wanted to seal his alliance with Assyria, he adjusted the temple contents to prove his intentions (2 Kings 16:10–18). His successor Hezekiah, on the other hand, wished to reassert Judah's independence, and set about removing such signs of external religious influence (2 Kings 18:1–7). Manasseh later brought them all back (2 Kings 21:1–18). Josiah eventually inaugurated a thoroughgoing religious reformation, and completely refurbished the temple as well as terminating local shrines throughout the country (2 Kings 23:1–20).

There was obviously a close connexion between the kings of Judah and the temple. Solomon played a major part in erecting the building and in organizing worship there. But he also had his own palace next door, linked to the temple by a private passage (2 Kings 16:18). The temple was more than a national place of worship: it also symbolized the power of the royal family of David. David and Solomon had political reasons for wanting to build a temple in Jerusalem. In the ancient world politics and religion were often two sides of the same coin. Various buildings mentioned on the

perimeter of the temple precinct may well have housed the king's personal treasury. Certainly, much of the nation's wealth must have been kept there, for invaders often went to the temple to plunder it (1 Kings 14:25–28; 15:15; 2 Kings 16:7–8; 18:15–16; 24:12–13).

As well as priests, the temple had a large staff, including administrators of various kinds (Ezra 2:40–42) and temple slaves who kept the fires burning on the various altars used in worship (Joshua 9:27; Ezra 2:43–54; 8:20). Some of these workers may well have been non-Israelites, for the prophet Ezekiel later complained about the practice of allowing foreigners to be involved in the life of the temple (Ezekiel 44:6–9).

Not everyone was happy with the temple. There were always radicals who felt that it was a backward step in Israel's spiritual pilgrimage, and that the covenant faith would be better served by adherence to the less settled ways of worship represented by the tent of the Lord's presence (2 Samuel 7:5–7; Jeremiah 35:1–19; Isaiah 66:1). But most people were committed to it. They knew well enough that God did not literally 'live' in the temple (Psalm 11:4; 1 Kings 8:27–30), but still this was the place where they felt most directly in God's presence (Psalm 63:1–5; 84:1–4; 122:1; 26:8). Their anguish was real and deeply felt when it was destroyed by the Babylonians (Psalm 137). After the exile, a replacement was built, of which we know only very little – but it was obviously a much less impressive place (Ezra 1:2–4; 3:1–6:18).

The synagogue

The exile was in many ways a great watershed for the people of Israel, and their worship was never again to be quite the same as it had been in the days of the great kings. The temple was rebuilt in Jerusalem, and it always had a special place in the affection of the Jewish people. But the effective centre of worship shifted to the synagogue. By the New Testament era there were synagogues in all the important towns of the Mediterranean world, and Jewish people went there week by week for regular worship.

Synagogue worship was quite different from temple worship. For one thing, it was on a much smaller scale. And in addition, it never included sacrifice. Prayer and the reading of the Old Testament Law and Prophets came to be all important. Naturally, there was no Ark of the Covenant or a holy of holies, though later synagogues had their own 'Ark of the Law' which contained the sacred scrolls of Scripture.

Almost all our evidence for life and worship in the synagogues is later than the Old Testament period – much of it a lot later. It shows the synagogues were more than places of worship: they were social and educational centres for the many Jewish communities scattered throughout the world in the early centuries of the Christian era. The synagogues emerged to fill a need which had not existed when Israel was an independent nation with their own land.

We have no real evidence to show how the synagogues originated. A number of ideas have been suggested:

● Some believe they began in Judah itself even before the exile. We know that in the course of his religious reforms, Josiah made a concerted effort to close down the local sanctuaries throughout his kingdom and to centralize all worship in Jerusalem. Of course, that could not eliminate the need for people to worship where they lived. And so, the argument goes, they went to Jerusalem only when they needed the sort of sacrificial worship that went on there. At other times they met for more informal local worship that was the forerunner of the synagogue. There is, however, no evidence to support this view. Indeed, it is doubtful whether Josiah's reformation was quite that successful, for less than twenty years later Jeremiah provides plenty of evidence of worship continuing at traditional sites throughout the country.

● It seems undeniable that the synagogue must have originated after the temple at Jerusalem was not available for worship. After the destruction of Jerusalem by Nebuchadnezzar, the remnants of the population left in Judah probably worshipped on the temple site from time to time (Jeremiah 41:4–5). But those who were transported to Babylon had no further access to Jerusalem. Possibly, therefore, synagogues first began as places of prayer and contemplation for these exiles in Babylon itself. We know these people certainly had a close interest in gathering together the books of the Law and Prophets. But here again there are no real facts to go on, and a certain amount of evidence to the contrary. In Psalm 137 the exiles bemoan their fate but with no reference at all to the possibility of synagogue worship. Archaeology has uncovered comparatively few remains of synagogue buildings in Babylon, none of them relating to the Old Testament period.

● It has also been suggested that the synagogue began in Palestine after the return of some of the exiles under Nehemiah and Ezra. There is a good deal of archaeological evidence for the existence of synagogue buildings in Palestine, though none of it goes back to this period. Perhaps the most we can say is that the need for regular worship, combined with the strong emphasis of Ezra on reading and interpretation of the Law (Nehemiah 8:1–12) could have provided the conditions for this new form of worship to evolve.

Wherever the synagogues came from, the simple worship carried on there was an authentic reflexion of an important strand in the Old Testament faith. For though the people rejoiced in the splendid magnificence of the temple at Jerusalem, it had always been recognized that God's presence could not be restricted to one place. The consciousness that God was with them (symbolized by the Ark of the Covenant) was more fundamental than the need for a holy place like the temple. There are many stories in the Old Testament which show that God's presence could be enjoyed anywhere. Joseph met God in a prison (Genesis 39:21), Jeremiah in a well (Jeremiah 38:1–13). When the Jewish people began to worship in synagogues throughout the world, not only were they coming to terms with the political realities of their national life: they were exploring new dimensions in the covenant faith itself. Perhaps that is why Jewish writers insisted that the synagogue began with Moses (Philo, *Life of Moses*, ii:39; Josephus, *Against Apion*, II:xvii. Historically, they were certainly wrong. But ideologically they were giving expression to an important aspect of the Old Testament faith.

The character of worship

What was worship like in Old Testament times? We have already referred in passing to prayer in the synagogue and sacrifice in the Jerusalem temple. Other passages mention the use of incense and

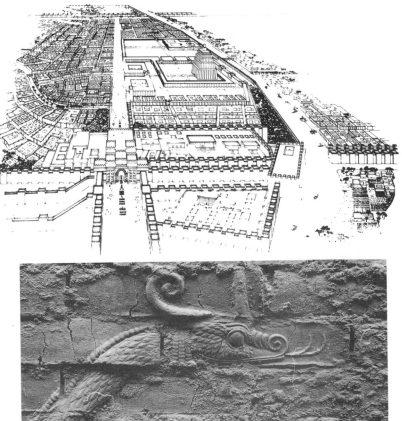

When the Jews were exiled in Babylon, they were surrounded by reminders of Babylonian mythology, like this dragon from Ishtar Gate (right). The whole city, shown in this artist's reconstruction (above right), was dominated by temples. Yet the Jews kept their own beliefs intact.

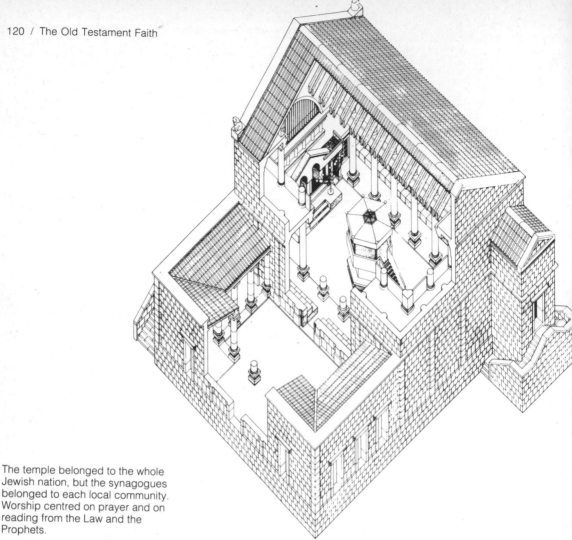

The temple belonged to the whole Jewish nation, but the synagogues belonged to each local community. Worship centred on prayer and on reading from the Law and the Prophets.

Jeremiah 6:20
Amos 4:4

Leviticus 1:1 — 7:38; Numbers
15:1–31; 28:1 — 29:40

the giving of monetary offerings. But the Old Testament never gives us a fully detailed account of a complete worship service. The most specific instructions refer to the offering of sacrifices, but worship obviously included a lot more than that. What went on in the local sanctuaries and in the temple was probably so familiar a part of life that it was unnecessary to spell it all out in detail. Of course, it was

The temple area in Jerusalem today has some remains of Herod's temple, built between 19 BC and AD 64. The original temple, known as Solomon's temple, was destroyed when the Babylonians sacked Jerusalem in 587 BC. The second temple was built after the Jews returned from exile in Babylon, and stood for almost 500 years.

These remains are of a synagogue at Capernaum. From the time when the Jews returned from Babylon, the synagogues began to play an important part in regular Jewish worship.

Old Testament worship had its services for the 'rites of passage' – birth, marriage and death. The box shown here is an ossuary, in which the deceased person's bones would have been interred. It dates from after the Old Testament period.

inevitable that the Old Testament should ignore some aspects of worship in ancient Israel. We know from the prophets that all too often the people worshipped their own God Yahweh using the rituals of the local Baal religion – and though this was popular, it was a denial of the true covenant faith.

In spite of the absence of any comprehensive set of instructions for the conduct of public worship, scholars agree that the Old Testament does contain a good deal of material that was regularly used in that context, especially in the book of Psalms. Some have called this 'the hymn book of the second temple'. It may well have been compiled at that time, for some psalms clearly refer to the exile and what followed. Not all psalms are hymns in the normal sense. Some of them are more personal and individual expressions of piety. Yet others refer to the great ceremonial events of national life. But whatever their form, the psalms give us an invaluable glimpse into the way God was worshipped in the temple at Jerusalem in the period before the exile. Sometimes we see individuals at worship. At others, we can catch sight of great national occasions involving the whole community. Some psalms centre on the king and God's promises to the royal family of David. One thing we do not find, however, is worship for the so-called 'rites of passage' – birth, marriage, and death. Most nations celebrate these events in the context of religious worship. But in ancient Israel they were all essentially family matters, and in the time before the exile they had no particular connexion with formal worship.

Understanding the psalms

At one time, scholars tried to understand the psalms either as purely personal poetry, or as poems composed on particular historical occasions in the course of Israel's history. But more recent study has suggested that most of them had their roots in the worship of Solomon's temple, and quite possibly in the worship at local sanctuaries as well. There are a number of reasons for accepting this:

● At least one Old Testament passage shows psalms being used in the course of worship. When David first brought the Ark of the Covenant into Jerusalem, its arrival was accompanied by dancing and singing (2 Samuel 6:5). One account of this incident includes an example of the songs that were sung on the occasion – and this turns out to be surprisingly similar to several of the psalms (1 Chronicles 16:8–36).

● Other Old Testament passages also confirm the important part played in worship by religious songs and poetry of the type found in the book of Psalms (Amos 5:23).

● Much of the imagery used in the psalms is very similar to imagery used in specifically religious poetry and songs elsewhere in the ancient Middle Eastern cultures. There are particularly close linguistic connexions between many of the psalms and the songs used to worship Baal as depicted in the texts from Ras Shamra. The theological ideas are completely different, of course, but a judicious comparison of the psalms with these other texts has led to enormous advances in our understanding of the meaning of many obscure Hebrew words used in the Old Testament.

● The Jerusalem temple and its worship provide many of the basic themes of the psalms, reflecting the centrality of the temple as a symbol of God's presence (Psalm 11:4; 46:4–6; 50:2) and the eager longing of the people to share in its worship (Psalm 26:8; 84:1–4; 122:1). Indeed, some of them even seem to refer directly to sacrificial worship (Psalm 36:8) and to the various days over which the great national festivals would be held (Psalm 118:24).

● The structure of some psalms seems to indicate that they were used as comprehensive liturgies for worship on particular occasions (Psalm 118:1–4). Some depict a number of participants in the worship, asking questions and receiving responses (Psalm 24). It is quite likely that many of the obscure references in the psalm titles are really instructions about how they were to be used in worship, and the Hebrew word *Selah* which appears in a number of psalms is almost certainly an instruction to the temple singers to increase the volume and sing louder.

Psalm 42 shows how much someone steeped in the worship at Jerusalem could miss the temple services. It is like drowning in the waterfalls of the Jordan submerged by 'waves of sorrow'.

When we analyze the psalms and other references to worship, we soon discover that it included many different activities.

Singing and music

1 Kings 18:27–29
1 Samuel 10:10–13
Amos 5:23
Psalm 22:3

Psalm 63:5
1 Chronicles 15:16–24; 16:4–7; Ezra 2:40–42

Psalm 42:5,11; 43:5; 46:7,11

2 Samuel 6:5; Psalm 43:4; 68:25; 81:1–3; 98:4–6; 150:3–5; Isaiah 30:29; 1 Chronicles 25:1–5

Psalm 42:4

This was a vital element in all worship, and it appears throughout the Old Testament as an appropriate way for God's people to praise him. It was, of course, an important activity in many ancient religions. When Elijah confronted the prophets of Baal on Mt Carmel, the Baal worshippers used music to stir themselves up into a frenzy. On occasion, prophets of Yahweh could use it for the same purpose. Not all religious singing was necessarily pleasing to God but without it his people could not truly praise him. His holy character found its natural response in this kind of worship, and the awareness of God's presence must inevitably lead to worshipping him in 'glad songs of praise'.

Singing became especially important after the exile, and the Old Testament mentions the names of several choirs in this connexion. Some of the psalms have refrains, which suggests that one part of the song would be sung by the worshippers, and the rest by the choir.

Musical instruments are mentioned in connexion with the praise of God: tambourines, harps, lyres, trumpets, rattles, horns, flutes, and cymbals. Worship was obviously a joyful business, and the carnival atmosphere of the temple is captured in one of the psalms which speaks of 'a happy crowd, singing and shouting praise to God'.

Prayer

This was to become one of the characteristic activities of the synagogue. By the New Testament period there were also regular daily times of prayer in the temple at Jerusalem. It is unclear whether this custom originated in Old Testament times, though prayer was certainly a vital element in worship right from the start. The belief that ordinary people could have direct access to God was a fundamental part of the Old Testament faith. Not only prophets such as Elijah, or kings such as Solomon, but ordinary people such as Hannah could bring their everyday problems to God. The Old Testament Law contains prayers to be said on special occasions, and the book of Psalms contains many examples of prayers that were no doubt used by individuals, as well as by groups of worshippers, to

1 Kings 18:36–37
1 Kings 8:22–61
1 Samuel 1:1–18
Deuteronomy 26:5–10

Music was important in the worship of Israel and her neighbours. The musicians above are from an Egyptian mural, and those in the picture centre right are Elamites (a relief from Ashurbanipal's palace in Nineveh). The cymbals are from Luristan (in modern Iran), but the photo far right shows a reconstruction of the kind of lyre King David would have played. But not all worship is music and singing; prayer is always central.

give thanks and to express their trust and confidence in God.

Sometimes the worshipper would kneel to pray, or even bow low to the ground. At other times prayers would be said in a standing position, occasionally with hands raised up above the head. But the important thing was not the posture for prayer, but 'a humble and repentant heart'.

1 Kings 8:54
Psalm 5:7
1 Samuel 1:26
1 Kings 8:22,54;
Psalm 63:4; Isaiah 1:15
Psalm 51:17

Dance and drama

Psalm 26:6
Psalm 149:3; 150:4

Given the importance attached to singing and music in Old Testament worship, we are not surprised to discover that dancing could also be used in praise of God. Some of the psalms seem to presuppose it, and others specifically encourage it. On one occasion even King David himself took part in public dancing as the Ark of

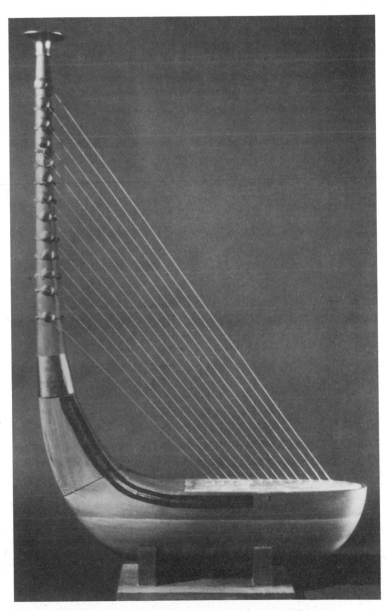

the Covenant was brought into his city of Jerusalem. Indeed, he danced so vigorously that his wife thought his behaviour was indecent, and rebuked him for making a fool of himself.

2 Samuel 6:1–22

There is also evidence for the use of drama in worship. There are many indications of processions in which the worshippers would march in and out of the temple and the city of Jerusalem. Sometimes, God is depicted accompanying the worshippers as they march – perhaps in the form of the Ark of the Covenant, carried at the head of the procession. Other passages suggest that God's mighty acts in the past could be re-enacted in the course of worship, to bring home their lessons to new generations. At the great annual Passover festival, drama also played an important part. At the most solemn moment of the festival, the worshippers ate a fellowship meal dressed ready to go on a journey, just as the slaves in Egypt had done at the time of the exodus. Symbolic actions could also play an important part in more ordinary acts of worship. Drama has always been a powerful medium through which people can express their deepest convictions, and when the worshippers of ancient Israel reminded themselves of God's goodness to their nation they did so in action as well as in word.

Psalm 26:6; 42:4; 48:12–14; 118:19,26–27

Psalm 68:24–27; 132:7–9

Psalm 46:8–10; 48:8; 66:5

Exodus 12:21–28
Psalm 26:6

Sacrifice

2 Kings 16:15

To many people, this is the most characteristic activity of Old Testament worship. Certainly, it was a daily ritual in the temple. But it was only one element among many. Modern Western people tend to give so much attention to it simply because it is generally remote from our own experience. To us, the gratuitous death of animals in the course of religious worship is something repugnant – and we are not aided here by the fact that the Old Testament never explains exactly why this form of worship was used. As with so many other things, it simply takes it for granted that everyone would know why sacrifice was an appropriate way to worship.

Sacrifice is a worldwide phenomenon, and is not restricted either to the Old Testament or the Middle East. Anthropologists have tried hard to understand the need for sacrifice in different cultural contexts around the world. To appreciate the importance of sacrifice, we need to return to the observations about 'holiness' with which we began this chapter. Wherever it is practised, sacrifice is always understood as a means of relating the visible, tangible world in which people exist to the invisible, intangible and uncontrollable world in which God or the gods exist. It is a means whereby people can encounter the powerful 'holiness' that radiates out from the presence of God, without suffering the horrific consequences that would normally follow such an encounter. This is why animals (particularly domestic animals) were appropriate as sacrifices, for they are themselves living, have a close relationship to people, and could therefore serve as a suitable symbol of the worshippers themselves.

A religion's view of God will always affect its view of sacrifice. In many primitive religions, sacrifice is thought of as a way of feeding the gods. But this is a view that the Old Testament rejects. The Old

Psalm 50:7–15

Testament's understanding of sacrifice is dominated by its perception of the meaning of holiness. This means that an important function of sacrifice was concerned with securing ritual purity. But the moral dimensions of God's holiness were never far from view. As time went on and the events of history made the need for forgiveness of sin more obvious, this came to be the predominant meaning attached to sacrifice.

Leviticus 11:1 — 15:33

Ezekiel 45:18–25

This does not mean, of course, that sacrifice and sin were related only at a late date. At an earlier period, even sacrifices that were not identified as 'sin offerings' could be accompanied by great repentance. The prophets and others often reminded the people of the need for true confession and repentance to accompany sacrificial worship. As in so many other things, the actual practice of ancient Israel varied from time to time and place to place. And there was always the temptation to offer sacrifices to gods other than Yahweh, using rituals that were fundamentally alien to the Old Testament faith.

Judges 20:26; 21:1–4; 1 Samuel 7:2–9; Job 1:5

Micah 6:6–8; Amos 5:21–24; Psalm 51:16–19

Jeremiah 44:24–25; Amos 5:25–27

The Old Testament mentions many different types of sacrifice. In some ways, they defy comprehensive analysis. But anthropologists have identified three major types of sacrifice, and it will be helpful to use these divisions in our discussion of the Old Testament.

● **Gift sacrifices** Sacrifices would often be given to God as a way of saying thank you for some particular benefit that the worshipper had received. The very first sacrifices mentioned in the Old Testament were of this type, as also was the sacrifice of Noah after the great flood had subsided. At the other end of the Old Testament story we find the exiles who returned from Babylon offering the same sort of sacrifices. They are also mentioned in many of the psalms.

Genesis 4:3–4
Genesis 8:20

Ezra 6:16–18
Psalm 54:6–7; 56:12–13

On other occasions, gift sacrifices would be offered in order to secure God's guidance for the future. But quite often a gift sacrifice would be given as a simple expression of joy on the part of the worshipper. Such offerings would usually be given in their entirety to God, by being burned on the altar of the sanctuary – hence the term sometimes used to describe them, 'whole burnt offerings'. Offerings of grain could also serve the same purpose, and the annual offerings of the first-fruits of the crops were in effect gift sacrifices given to celebrate a successful harvest.

1 Samuel 7:9

1 Samuel 6:14; 2 Samuel 6:17; Psalm 96:8

Leviticus 1:1–17
Leviticus 2:1–16

Leviticus 23:1–25

● **Fellowship offerings** Not all sacrifices were given completely to God as whole burnt offerings. Often, only a part of the animal was burned on the altar, and the rest was eaten in a fellowship meal at the sanctuary, shared by worshippers and priests. A shared meal is a symbol of friendship throughout the world. But the worshippers of ancient Israel were doing more than simply expressing their mutual affection. For the most important event of their history, the covenant ceremony at Mt Sinai, had been accompanied by a fellowship offering like this. Whenever this event was celebrated a fellowship offering was usually at the centre of things. No doubt the same themes would be in the worshippers' minds whenever fellowship offerings were made. In these meals the people were constantly

Leviticus 3:1–17

Exodus 24:1–8
Joshua 8:30–35; 2 Samuel 6:17; 1 Kings 8:63–64

reminded of the keynote of their covenant faith: that God and his people enjoyed a personal relationship whose repercussions influenced the whole of life.

● **Forgiveness of sins** The Old Testament mentions two sacrifices that were designed to remove the barrier of sin that made fellowship between people and God impossible: the sin offering and the guilt offering. The precise difference between these two classes of sacrifice is not very clear. But in view of the way that God's holiness was equated with moral perfection, it is not surprising that sacrifice and forgiveness should have been related to each other. Human sin broke the covenant relationship between God and his people. But fellowship could be restored by offering an appropriate sacrifice.

An awareness of the seriousness of sin seems to have developed most fully in the later stages of Israel's history. The earlier prophets often found it difficult to convince the people that worship and behaviour belonged together. But when the awful events of the exile had proved them right, everyone could see that disobedience to God was a real problem that needed to be dealt with. The Old Testament never specifically discusses how a sacrifice could deal with sin. But it is clear that it was taken for granted that those who sinned deserved to die, and that a sacrifice in some way substituted for the condemned sinner. Certainly, the blood of these sacrifices (representing the life of the animal) played an important part. It was only as this was daubed on the altar that the worshipper could be pronounced forgiven. Depending on the identity of the sinner, different altars could be used.

There was one occasion when the whole nation was united in seeking forgiveness: the annual Day of Atonement. On this occasion, the blood of the sacrifices would be taken into the holy of holies itself, and applied to the top of the Ark. This was why the lid of the Ark came to be known as 'the mercy seat'. After the exile it was replaced by a gold plate which served the same purpose. When the

Leviticus 4:1 — 5:13

Leviticus 5:14 — 6:7; Numbers 5:5–8

Ezekiel 18:20

Leviticus 17:11

Leviticus 16:1–34; 23:26–32; Numbers 29:7–11

main sacrifices had been offered, a second ritual took place. This involved the selection of two goats, one to be sacrificed in the temple and the other to be sent away into the desert beyond the inhabited land. The priest laid his hands on the head of the goat which was to be sent out and confessed the sins of the nation. These two procedures were quite different, but they both emphasized the same facts: that sin is a serious business as it disrupts fellowship between God and his people. They were also a dramatic declaration that sin could be forgiven, and removed from the lives of God's people as surely as the goat was driven out into the desert, never to be seen again.

Understanding sacrifice

So far, we have looked at the ways in which sacrifices were used in the worship of God in the Old Testament. But what is sacrifice all about? Just what did the worshippers think they were doing when they engaged in this sort of activity? At one time, it was thought that sacrifice was based on superstition and ignorance, and that it was only relatively late in Israel's history that it came to have any theological significance, as sacrifice became a way of making amends for sin. But modern anthropologists studying sacrifice in

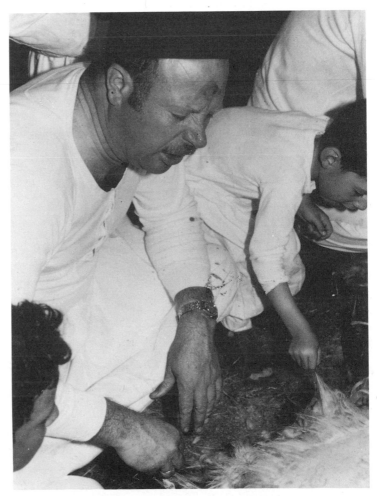

Israel and her neighbours sacrificed animals as part of their worship. The sacrificial animals being carried in procession (left) are from a relief at Carchemish on the upper Euphrates; the sacrifices on the right are being made by the small group of Samaritans who remain today; and the horned altar below was probably used for Israelite burnt offerings.

many different cultures have shown that, whatever else it is, sacrificial worship certainly is not unsophisticated.

Wherever it is practised, sacrifice is a means of reaffirming the structures of civilized life: it declares that God and people are united in a relationship of mutual interdependence, and, by means of the meal which often follows a sacrifice, it affirms the importance of good social relationships as a basis for a contented life. In the context of the Old Testament faith, those affirmations are central. Peace and harmony with God is a fundamental requirement for a good life – and peace and harmony both in nature and in human society stem only from God himself. Sacrifice, therefore, needed to be offered at those points in a person's life when they were out of tune with the 'holiness' which characterized God's own being.

Sacrifice and holiness

Just as God's holiness was defined in a number of ways, so sacrifices could be offered for a number of purposes.

● In relation to the mysterious, numinous holiness that radiated out from the divine presence, sacrifice was the means by which a person who was 'unclean' could be made 'clean' and fit to encounter God's holy power. In this context, the notion of 'unclean' was not related to morality or behaviour. Things

Different kinds of sacrifice

Category of sacrifice	Example of category	How sacrifice conducted	Spiritual meaning
Gift sacrifices	Firstfruits Grain offerings Offerings in thanks for particular blessings	Burnt in entirety on the altar (whole burnt offerings)	Gratitude to God Joy in him
Fellowship offerings	Events of national significance e.g. sealing covenant, dedicating temple, covenant renewal	Part burnt, part eaten in fellowship meal with priests and worshippers	Reminder of covenant relationship with God
Sacrifices for forgiveness of sins	Sin offerings Guilt offerings Sacrifice on Day of Atonement	Blood daubed on the altar	Animal is dying in place of sinner

such as illness, touching a dead body, giving birth, menstruation, even having mildew in the houses or clothing, all rendered a person 'unclean' in a ritual sense (Leviticus 11–15). To us, this seems rather an odd collection of things. But what unites them seems to be the fact that they are all things that happen occasionally, and are not a part of everyday life. In this context, those things that are 'clean' are perhaps what we might call 'normal' – and any unusual occurrence renders a person 'unclean'. The precise reasons for this are no doubt lost in the mists of antiquity. But before a person could approach the holy presence of God in the sanctuary, such uncleanness had to be dealt with by the offering of appropriate sacrifices.

● There was also a moral side to God's holiness. Wrongdoing also made people 'unclean', and therefore unfit to deal with God. An inadequate understanding of this led to many problems in the history of ancient Israel. The people were naturally inclined to think that worship was concerned only with the ritual aspects of holiness – and the prophets were continually reminding them that ritual worship and everyday behaviour could not be separated. There can be no doubt the nation as a whole took a long time to learn this lesson – and that is the reason why offerings for sin came to assume more importance as time went on. For sacrifice was also the way that sin could be forgiven, and people could be restored to fellowship with God.

Making a sacrifice

The worshipper who made a sacrifice in ancient Israel did so out of a consciousness of being alienated from God, for whatever reason. Reconciliation with God had to be achieved in order for life to proceed as God intended it to be. This sense of alienation is familiar enough to modern people. Modern Christians would tend to place all the emphasis on internal spiritual change as the means of overcoming it. But in the Old Testament, this change of internal disposition was always displayed externally. Here, sacrifice became a visible symbol of change in a person's life. We can trace a number of stages in the process whereby this change was

brought about.

First of all, the sinner would approach the altar of God with the sacrifice. He then laid his hand on the animal's head, to indicate that he wished to be identified with the animal. This was most important, for it meant that from this point onwards the animal was to be a symbol of the worshipper: whatever happened physically and outwardly to the animal was to happen to the worshipper spiritually and inwardly. Four things then took place:

● The animal was killed. In this action, the worshipper was reminded of the consequence of uncleanness: death, separation from fellowship with God. The worshipper himself would perform this action, declaring that he was fit only for death himself.

● The priest then took the blood of the sacrifice (which now represented the sinner's life given up to God) to the altar. Depending on the identity of the sinner, different altars would be used. For an ordinary person, it was the altar of burnt offerings in the temple courtyard; for a priest, the altar of incense in the temple itself; and for the whole nation (on the Day of Atonement), the lid of the Ark in the holy of holies. This action constituted the moment when the worshipper's uncleanness was removed (Leviticus 17:11) – the moment of reconciliation, or 'atonement' as it is sometimes called. God and his people had been reunited in fellowship.

● After this, the animal's body was placed on the altar in the temple, as a sign that the forgiven sinner was offering his whole life to God. In the case of a gift offering, the whole sacrifice would be burned there.

● Finally, depending on the nature of the sacrifice, some of the meat still left was eaten in a meal. Not only were things right between God and the individual worshipper: true fellowship with other people had also been restored.

We can see from all this that sacrifice was a very important part of worship. It both represented basic aspects of the Old Testament faith (people made for fellowship with God and with one another), and also externalized the faith in such a way that no one would be left in any doubt about what it meant to address Yahweh as a holy God.

Times for worship

We have already seen that worship involved a whole style of life, including daily behaviour as well as what went on at the sanctuaries. It was, therefore, a continuous activity. One of the major themes of the Old Testament faith is that God is available to people at every time and in every place. Formal worship was one way of expressing this, and the sanctuaries would be open every day. But there were also special times when the great national festivals would interrupt the normal run of things and the people would join together to celebrate God's goodness to them. The significance of the different festivals changed with the passage of time, but we can trace a number of important occasions in the Old Testament.

The sabbath day

Many nations in the ancient world had a regular day of rest, and the celebration of the sabbath every seventh day was an important part of Old Testament life from a very early date. There is no single passage which describes what a sabbath should be like. But it probably began as a day of rest, so that every member of the population (including slaves and foreigners) could renew themselves for their daily work. Worship was a part of this renewal process, and no doubt it was an occasion when crowds would throng to the various sanctuaries throughout the land – though what they did there was not always pleasing to God. On the sabbath, no regular work would be undertaken, though it would not necessarily be a day of complete rest for everyone.

Exodus 23:12; 34:21

Leviticus 19:30; Numbers 28:9–10
Isaiah 1:13; 2:11
Amos 8:5; Jeremiah 17:21–22
2 Kings 11:5–8

The main emphasis was on the sabbath as a day to look back to the nation's roots, to celebrate God's goodness and greatness, and to renew a commitment to the covenant faith. This is no doubt why its observance is required in the Ten Commandments. The whole day was specially dedicated to God ('holy'), because it was a reminder of his greatness both in creation and history. It was also a reminder to them that belief in God meant concern for other people. In the period after the Babylonian exile, the sabbath became very important in the synagogues. Eventually it became a day that was rigidly controlled by many prohibitions. But in the Old Testament period it was a day for joyful celebration.

Exodus 20:8–11
Exodus 31:12–17
Exodus 20:11; Deuteronomy 5:15
Deuteronomy 5:13–14

Isaiah 58:13–14

The Passover

The greatest event of all to which the people looked back was God's deliverance of the slaves from Egypt (the exodus). This was marked in an annual festival at which an animal was sacrificed, and a meal was shared. In this respect, the Passover was just a special form of fellowship offering, celebrating the relationship inaugurated between God and people in the exodus events. These events themselves had a profound impact on the way the festival was celebrated. The people dressed up in the same way as their ancestors had done – 'with your sandals on your feet and your stick in your hand' – as if ready for a long journey.

Exodus 12:11

According to the story of the exodus, the people prepared to leave Egypt in their family groups. This is how the Passover was celebrated in the earlier part of the Old Testament period. A lamb was sacrificed in the home, with none of the splendour of worship found in the sanctuaries. The animal's blood was daubed not on an altar but on the doorposts of the house. At this time, the animal was always a lamb roasted for the fellowship meal – a custom perhaps

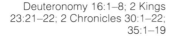

The great Old Testament festivals have carried over into modern Judaism. This Jewish family are celebrating Passover, recalling their ancestors' deliverance from slavery in Egypt.

Deuteronomy 16:1–8; 2 Kings 23:21–22; 2 Chronicles 30:1–22; 35:1–19

Deuteronomy 16:2
Deuteronomy 16:7

Numbers 9:1–14; 2 Chronicles 30:23–27

Exodus 1 — 15
Exodus 15:1–18

going back to the origin of the festival in the days when Israel had been a nomadic sheep-rearing people. Later, it became a national occasion, centred on the temple in Jerusalem, with all the impressive pageantry associated with worship there. The ritual naturally changed to suit the different circumstances. Both sheep and cattle could be used in the celebrations, boiled rather than roasted. There was also a provision whereby anyone who missed the Passover because they were ritually unclean could celebrate it a month later than the proper date. It has been suggested that the worshippers in the temple may have recited the story of the first Passover and exodus, perhaps acting out the events and culminating with the singing of the great 'song of Moses'.

In the New Testament period, both the family and the national elements of the occasion were united. The sacrifices were killed in the temple but the fellowship meals then eaten in a family home.

The harvest festivals

Exodus 23:14–17; 34:18–23

The Old Testament mentions three major religious festivals that relate to the agricultural year. These celebrations had probably always been a part of the national life of the inhabitants of Canaan. Similar occasions are celebrated by farmers all over the world. But the Old Testament links each of them to the great and unrepeatable events of Israel's history, not to the cycle of the seasons and the inevitable concern of farmers for the continuing fertility of their land.

Leviticus 23:9–14; Numbers 28:10–23

● **The festival of Unleavened Bread** was apparently related to the barley harvest and the offering of the first-fruits. But this was celebrated at the same time of year as Passover and that, together with the fact that unleavened bread features in the passover story, meant that the two festivals came to be closely connected, and together served to commemorate the escape from Egypt.

Numbers 28:26–31

Leviticus 23:15–21

● **The Corn Harvest** (or Feast of Weeks) celebrated the end of the wheat harvest. Special offerings would be made in the sanctuaries, though the central action was the ceremonial presentation of the first sheaf that had been cut. Following this, individual worshippers could bring offerings from their own crops. The events

Festivals of the Jewish Year

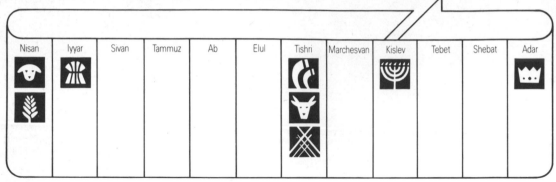

Nisan	Iyyar	Sivan	Tammuz	Ab	Elul	Tishri	Marchesvan	Kislev	Tebet	Shebat	Adar

 Passover (evening)/**Unleavened Bread** (whole week). Remembering deliverance from Egypt

 Firstfruits (last day of Unleavened Bread). First sheaf of barley harvest presented to God

 Weeks/Pentecost (fifty days after Passover). Rejoicing for corn harvest

 Trumpets/New Year (first day of seventh month). Tishri celebrated as specially solemn month

 Day of Atonement (ten days after Trumpets). Day of national repentance and fasting; in Old Testament, annual sacrifice and scapegoat

Shelters/Tabernacles (at end of fruit harvests). Families camped out in shelters for a week

Dedication/Lights (began after Old Testament period). Celebrated cleansing of second temple

Purim (another festival of later origin) Recalls story of Esther

Three other celebrations were not annual:

Sabbath Seventh day of each week kept as special day of rejoicing

Sabbatical Year Every seventh year, ground intended to lie fallow

Jubilee Year Every fiftieth year, all property intended to revert to original owner or descendants

---

Deuteronomy 16:12

Leviticus 23:33–43; Deuteronomy 16:13–17

of the exodus were also in the minds of the worshippers on this occasion, though after the exile the harvest festival came to be used as a time for celebrating the giving of the Law at Mt Sinai.

● **The Festival of Shelters** (or Tabernacles) came at the very end of the growing season, and was a celebration of the fruit harvest from vineyards and orchards. This was a particularly joyful festival,

The Festival of Shelters is in direct continuity with the Jews of Ezra's day. As well as celebrating the fruit and vine harvest, it reminds participants of the Israelites' wilderness days and the beginning of their covenant faith.

and took its character from the practice of the farmers, who would stay out all night to guard their crops, with only flimsy huts to protect them. For the seven days of the festival, the worshippers lived in similar structures.

The main feature of this occasion was the simple expression of joy at the safe gathering of the harvest. But there also seems to be a close connexion between the Festival of Shelters and the renewal of the covenant faith. The Old Testament identifies the temporary shelters with the tents in which Israel lived in the desert. Some have suggested that this association only came in later, when the shelters traditionally used at this time of year no longer had any practical relevance to the essentially non-agricultural life of the exiles. But many more are of the opinion that the covenant theme was always an important part of this festival, even from the earliest days of Israel's life in the land of Canaan. Allegiance to the covenant certainly seems to have been the bond that united the various tribes in the days of the judges. It is likely that they renewed their commitment to God and to one another in annual ceremonies which would include the reading of the covenant law. The Old Testament indicates that this covenant law could be read out as a part of the Festival of Shelters, and many scholars therefore believe that this would be followed by a solemn moment when the people committed themselves once again to the demands of God's covenant and his Law.

Leviticus 23:33–44

Exodus 24:7; Deuteronomy 27:9–10; Joshua 24:1–28

Deuteronomy 31:9–13; Nehemiah 8:13–18

Old Testament worship was a varied experience. But one thing we do not find in it is preaching. After the exile the *Torah* was regularly expounded during organized worship. But in the earlier Old Testament period, the main emphasis was always on praise and celebration. Like daily behaviour, worship was a response to God as he had made himself known in the events of Israel's history and the everyday experience of ordinary people. As the joyful worshippers went to the sanctuaries, they were reminded of God's past goodness, and given fresh inspiration for their own lives. But they were also challenged by his holiness, as they faced the central need for repentance and forgiveness – and offered sacrifices in order to secure it. As time went on, it was this repetitive nature of much Old Testament worship that led prophets and others to question its lasting effectiveness, and to see it as but one stage on the road to a closer relationship with God. Could God not forgive sin in a more comprehensive way, they asked, so that his people could really praise him as men and women 'pure in act and thought'?

Nehemiah 8:7–9

Psalm 24:4

The Old Testament never really gives an answer to that question, though some of its writers looked forward to a time when the covenant would be renewed in such a way that the past would be forgiven, and the future could hold out the hope of real victory over the power of evil. They never spelled out the meaning of that in detail. But they were sure that God could be trusted to work for the benefit of the whole world, which he had made and on which he set his love. When men and women commit themselves to God in humble trust, whether it be in great corporate acts of worship or in

Jeremiah 31:31–34

the private recesses of their own lives, they will always learn more about the true meaning of life and faith:

> Don't you know? Haven't you heard?
> The Lord is the everlasting God;
> he created all the world.
> He never grows tired or weary.
> No one understands his thoughts.
> He strengthens those who are weak and tired.
> Even those who are young grow weak;
> young men can fall exhausted.
> But those who trust in the Lord for help
> will find their strength renewed.
> They will rise on wings like eagles;
> they will run and not get weary;
> they will walk and not grow weak.

Isaiah 40:28–31

Kings, priests and prophets in worship

The existence of a regular system for public worship inevitably requires full time officials to look after the places of worship, and to supervise what goes on there. In the Old Testament a number of figures appear to be important in this connexion.

The Kings

Throughout the ancient Middle East, kings had a special role in religion. Their precise function varied from place to place. In Egypt, for example, the pharaoh was often thought to be himself a divine being. In Babylon, on the other hand, he was more often regarded as a sort of messenger of the gods – an intermediary between people and gods, though not himself divine. Although some have argued otherwise, it is unlikely that the kings of either Israel or Judah were ever thought of as gods themselves. Indeed, when the Syrian Naaman assumed that one of them was a god, he was quick to disclaim it (2 Kings 5:7). The psalms contain ample evidence to show that the people prayed not to the king, but to God on his behalf (Psalm 20:1–9; 72:1–19). From the earliest days of Israel's arrival in the land of Canaan, God himself had always been regarded as the king. The tension between this belief and the political need for a military leader was recognized in the stories of Saul's appointment (1 Samuel 8:1–22; 10:17–27), and occasionally features in the message of the prophets (Hosea 8:4). But even when the idea of kingship was accepted, God himself was still regarded as the supreme sovereign of his people, and the king as his servant (Deuteronomy 17:14–20).

The special nature of the king's position was symbolized in the fact that he was anointed. This ritual signified his close relationship with God, and declared that he was, in effect, a 'holy' person. David recognized this quality even in Saul (1 Samuel 24:5–7), and when Saul was killed in the heat of battle his murderer had to be punished for killing 'the one whom the Lord had chosen to be king' (2 Samuel 1:14–16). This special relationship between God and the king was expressed in the idea of a 'covenant' existing between God, the royal family of David, and the people of Judah (2 Samuel 7:8–16), and the king could on occasion even be called God's 'son' (Psalm 2:7).

The king could also be called a priest (Psalm 110:4). Kings in general often had an important part to play in organized worship, and the Old Testament depicts the kings of Israel and Judah engaged in such activities. Throughout the whole history of both kingdoms, the kings played an important part in public worship. David established centres of worship (2 Samuel 6:17; 24:25), and Solomon, of course, built the temple itself (1 Kings 5:1–6:14). The first king of the northern kingdom of Israel also set up sanctuaries in his own land, and decreed the sort of worship that should be carried out there (1 Kings 12:26–33). As a result, these shrines were thought of as 'the king's place of worship, the national temple' (Amos 7:13). But the same was true of the temple in Jerusalem, for the kings of Judah controlled the worship there too. The priests were effectively members of the royal household, under the control of the king (2 Samuel 8:17; 20:25; 1 Kings

'Those who trust in the Lord for help will find their strength renewed. They will rise on wings like eagles' (Isaiah 40:31).

2:26–35; 4:4; 2 Kings 12:4–16). The kings also took charge of religious policy-making. Asa (1 Kings 15:11–15), Ahaz (2 Kings 16:1–18), Joash (2 Kings 12:1–19), Hezekiah (2 Kings 18:1–7), Manasseh (2 Kings 21:1–9) and Josiah (2 Kings 22:3–23:23) are all specifically credited with having reorganized temple worship in one way or another.

As well as being responsible for the general tenor of organized worship, the kings could also on occasion conduct worship. Saul (1 Samuel 13:8–10; 14:35), David (2 Samuel 6:13; 24:25), Solomon (1 Kings 3:3–4; 8:62–63), Jeroboam 1 (1 Kings 12:32—13:1) and Ahaz (2 Kings 16:1–16) all offered sacrifices regularly. Kings could also pray on behalf of the nation, and issue blessings in God's name (1 Kings 8:14–66; 2 Kings 19:14–19). On one occasion, David offered sacrifice and gave a blessing while clothed in the apparel of a priest (2 Samuel 6:12–19).

The kings obviously had an important role in the religious life of their people. Since they were believed to be appointed by God, this is not surprising, for they had the power to encourage their people to maintain the covenant faith – and, on occasion, to corrupt it. There have been many arguments as to the precise nature of the kingship, in view of the many 'priestly' functions that kings could carry out. But a number of factors suggest that we need to be cautious in claiming that the king's main function was religious rather than political:

● Religion and politics were always closely related in the ancient world. In particular, the various superpowers of the day often imposed their own religions on their vassals, as a means of demonstrating the vassals' subservience. This fact alone explains why the kings of Judah were so often involved in changing the equipment used in the temple. Restoration of the covenant faith meant reasserting Judah's independence.

● The exclusive functions of the priests were not so well defined during the time of the monarch as they were later to become after the exile. As we shall see below, any head of the family could offer sacrifices or establish a new place of worship – and when the kings engaged in such activities they could well have been acting mainly in that capacity.

● It is perhaps significant that the only occasions when we have specific reports of kings conducting worship were particularly important times in the life of the nation. Even today, monarchs

tend to be involved in religious celebrations at important moments, although they themselves have no regular 'priestly' functions. No doubt, in general, the day to day conduct of worship in ancient Israel would be left in the hands of other religious officials, appointed by the king for the job.

Priests

We have already seen that during the period of the monarchy the priests often had a close relationship with the king himself. Some experts have suggested that the priesthood itself only emerged at this period. But its existence and functions must go back further than that.

It is certainly true that the Old Testament shows a lot of flexibility in worship at an earlier time. A number of stories show the heads of families offering sacrifices (Genesis 22:13; 31:54; 46:1; Judges 6:19–27; 13:19–23; 1 Samuel 1:3; 2:12–13; 9:12–13). But this is not of itself evidence that there were no priests, for even much later the actual act of sacrifice was always performed by the worshipper himself and not by the priest.

More surprising, perhaps, is the way that in this early period it was apparently possible for clans and other groups to appoint and dismiss their own priests at will (Judges 17:1–18:31). But incidents of this kind may well have been exceptions, for it would be odd if Israel had no organized priesthood at this time. Other nations certainly had well developed priesthoods, and the Old Testament mentions some of them: the Canaanite priest Melchizedek (Genesis 14:17–24), the Egyptian priest Potiphera (Genesis 41:45–46), the Midianite Jethro (Exodus 18:1), and the Philistine priests of Dagon (1 Samuel 5:5). In the context of the religious ideas of the time, the existence of the Ark of the Covenant and the tent of the Lord's presence almost necessitate the existence of professional priests to take care of them.

So what did priests do, and how did they operate? The answer to that question naturally changed with the years. After the exile, with the disappearance of the kings, the priests came to occupy an important political place. But in the earlier period, they must have operated in a more restricted religious capacity, at least in the great national sanctuaries that were closely controlled by the kings. Some aspects of their work are unclear, especially the relationship between priests and

Levites. But the Old Testament gives information about several of their functions.

● Priests cared for the sanctuaries throughout the land (Judges 17:1–13; 1Samuel 1–3:21; Amos 7:10–13). They would get their living from the gifts of worshippers – and, of course, they also had their share of the meat from the sacrifices (Numbers 18:8–32; 1 Samuel 2:12–16). They could also have their own lands and property (1 Kings 2:26; Amos 7:17).

● People would also consult the priests in order to get advice for particular situations. One story tells how Saul first met Samuel while he was asking for advice about some lost donkeys (1 Samuel 9:3–16). The account does not tell us precisely how Saul expected Samuel to know where they were, but other passages seem to imply that the priest would use a set of special dice (Urim and Thummim) to give the answer to such questions (1 Samuel 14:41–42; Deuteronomy 33:8; Exodus 28:30). It is not known exactly how this procedure operated, but it seems to have died out quite early in any case. After the time of David, it is the prophets who give direct advice and instruction of this kind (1 Kings 20:13–14; 22:6; 2 Kings 3:11–19).

● More generally, the priests would give instructions (*Torah*) on questions relating to worship. They were able to pronounce on whether things, places or people were clean or unclean, holy or profane, and so give guidance to the worshippers (Leviticus 10:8–11; 13:1–8; Ezekiel 22:26; 44:23; Haggai 2:11–14). Some scholars believe that moral law such as the Ten Commandments may also have been 'preached' in this way by the priests. After the exile, the Levites had the job of teaching. But their *'Torah'* was different from the earlier priestly teaching, since it now consisted of exposition of parts of the written Old Testament books (Nehemiah 8:7–9). Priests could also have certain judicial functions, as we saw in a previous chapter.

Priests were involved in the offering of sacrifices. It would be the worshipper who actually killed the animal. But the priest gave advice about the appropriate form of sacrifice to be offered on different occasions, and it was always the priest (as a specially 'holy' person) who took the blood to the altar. In this context, he was a mediator – representing God to the people, and the people to God.

● The priest could also mediate between God and people when he gave answers in God's name to the prayers of the worshippers (1 Samuel 1:17), or pronounced a blessing upon them (Numbers 6:22–26).

It was this function as mediator which was most characteristic of the priest's work. He was specially consecrated to God, and as such was able to deal with the awesome holiness of a place of worship. Through his presence, God and people could be brought together in a tangible way.

Prophets

When the people of Jerusalem were plotting to get rid of Jeremiah, they commented that even if they disposed of him, 'There will always be priests to instruct us, wise men to give us counsel, and prophets to proclaim God's message' (Jeremiah 18:18). At one time, scholars were surprised to see prophets and priests mentioned in the same breath, as if they were complementary to each other. A hundred years ago it was an 'assured result' of Old Testament study that priests and prophets were implacably opposed to each other. They represented different kinds of religion: priests being concerned with the arid and mechanical performance of pointless ritual, and prophets with the communication of a vital and life-giving message from God. It was widely supposed that the great Old Testament prophets were moral preachers, with no interest in organized religion at all – and it was only after the exile that a lesser breed of prophets emerged, who then became involved in formal worship because the fire of the original prophetic message had been all but extinguished.

It is certainly true that some of the prophets were outspoken in their criticism of empty formality (Amos 5:21–24; Hosea 6:6; Micah 6:6–8; Isaiah 1:10–17). But we can now see that it was wrong to dissociate them altogether from the cult. Closer Old Testament study has shown that the prophets as a group often were closely linked with organized worship. A number of factors have led to this conclusion:

● As we have seen throughout this book, formal worship and everyday behaviour were closely linked in the Old Testament faith. Both of them were part of the people's response to God's goodness. The prophets could not have denied outright the importance of organized worship without also denying the very foundations of the covenant faith.

● The general picture often shows

This reconstruction of a Jewish high priest's breastplate shows twelve stones with symbols for the twelve tribes of Israel.

priests and prophets working alongside each other. Samuel and Elijah are the only prophets whom we know carried out priestly functions (1 Samuel 7:9; 11:15; 1 Kings 18:36–39). But other passages connect them quite clearly (Jeremiah 5:31; 23:11; 26:7,16; 29:26; Lamentations 2:20; Zechariah 7:1–3). And we know of at least one prophet who had his own room in the temple at Jerusalem (Jeremiah 35:3–4).

● The prophets often delivered their messages in the context of organized worship, and their themes were often related to the great festivals. For example, when Amos spoke of the coming 'Day of the Lord', he was probably taking up the popular expectations in the mind of the worshippers as they approached the climax of one of the great festivals – though Amos turned their expectations upside down (Amos 5:18–24). When the priest Amaziah challenged Amos, he

suggested that he should go and proclaim his message somewhere else, because he could not expect to be employed in Bethel – thus implying that prophets would on occasion be employed there (Amos 7:10–13). Then we also need to take account of the fact that both Jeremiah (Jeremiah 1:1) and Ezekiel (Ezekiel 1:1) were themselves members of priestly families.

Observations of this kind have been taken to indicate that Jeremiah, Ezekiel and others were actually on the staff at various places of worship. But there is no real evidence to support that. The evidence only shows them in the temple to speak and to attend worship. In a later age, Jesus did both – but no one ever thought he was a priest! It was just good sense to go where the people were, and to use familiar motifs to present a message. In any case, the prophets never restricted their preaching to cultic occasions, but went

Several prophets compared themselves to watchmen in their watchtowers, set to give warning when the people left God's ways. The prophets hated empty, formalized worship with no moral content.

into the market-place, the fields, and anywhere else that people would listen.

● Certain psalms seem to imply that someone spoke in the name of God during the liturgy of worship. A number of psalms that begin as lamentation end in thanksgiving – implying that at some point during the prayer the worshipper has been reassured of God's continuing presence (Psalm 20; 22; 86). Others contain such messages of reassurance said to have come direct from God himself (Psalm 12:5; 85:9–13; 91:14–16). One psalm clearly says that such messages were delivered by 'an unknown voice' in the course of temple worship (Psalm 81:5–16). We have seen that worship often included drama, and since other parts of the Old Testament show the prophets to be speakers on God's behalf, who better than a 'cultic

prophet' of this kind to play such a part in worship?

There is some evidence for this in the work of the Chronicler, who in one passage gives the title 'Levites' to people who were designated 'prophets' in the earlier account of Kings (compare 2 Chronicles 34:30 with 2 Kings 23:2). In other passages, these same 'Levites' are expressly given prophetic functions, including the deliverance of messages on God's behalf during worship (1 Chronicles 25:1–6; 2 Chronicles 20:13–19). Scholars have naturally speculated on the exact tasks performed by such cultic prophets. Unfortunately, apart from these rather vague references in Chronicles, and the implications of certain psalms, there is no specific information to help us further.

6 The Old and the New

The problem

THE OLD Testament has always been highly important for Christians: it is quoted on nearly every page of the New. And yet it has also presented them with a problem, and even in the very earliest days of the church its meaning and relevance were subjects of heated debate and controversy. In the years immediately following the death and resurrection of Jesus, this was the one issue that caused most friction and dissension in the lives of the young churches. Jesus himself had claimed that his own life was a 'fulfilment' of the Old Testament. Yet many of his actions seemed to set aside its most distinctive teachings, especially on subjects such as sabbath-keeping and the food laws, but also some of its moral teaching. What kind of authority then should the Old Testament have in the lives of Jesus' followers?

Matthew 5:17
Mark 2:23–28
Mark 7:14–23
Matthew 5:21–48

The very first generation of Christians were also Jews, and for them there was no particular problem. For the most part they continued to observe the way of life in which they had been brought up, based on the Old Testament as it was understood in first-century Judaism. But once it became clear that the Christian message was for non-Jewish people, and that Romans and Greeks could also become followers of Jesus Christ, the question of the Old Testament's authority presented itself in an altogether more pressing form. Was it necessary for a Gentile person to become a Jew in order to be a Christian? Paul and other New Testament writers answered that question with a firm 'no'. But they still kept the Old Testament as their sacred scriptures, and often used these ancient books as a basis for their own exposition of the Christian faith.

Galatians; 1 Peter; Hebrews

And therein lies the problem. For if certain parts of the Old Testament can be set aside as no longer relevant to Christian faith and action, how can we tell which those bits are – and what should we do with the rest of it?

Searching for solutions

The question of the relationship between Old Testament and New was put in an outspoken way by a second-century Christian called Marcion. Not only did he see the ambiguities in the position evidently taken by the apostles. He also noted other problems for Christian belief in the Old Testament. Jesus had spoken of a God of love who was concerned for the well-being of all men and women. But as Marcion read the Old Testament he often saw there a rather different picture of God, in which he seemed to be associated with extreme savagery and cruelty. Far from seeking the salvation of people, he sometimes seemed to be associated with their annihilation. Of course, Marcion had the picture slightly out of focus: stern judgment was an important part of Jesus' teaching, and God's love was never absent from the Old Testament faith, as we have seen in many different ways.

Nevertheless, modern readers have often felt the same way, and some Christians today would find it difficult to reconcile some aspects of the Old Testament's view of God with what they take to be the mainstream Christian view of the New Testament. As well as the matters to which Marcion drew attention, they might also refer to the contrast between the universal message of God's love in Isaiah 40–55 and the apparently narrow-minded nationalism of a book such as Ezra. And even the most ingenious interpreter would find it exceedingly difficult to reconcile the sentiments of Psalm 137 with the statements about loving enemies in Jesus' Sermon on the Mount (Matthew 5:43–48). Then again, many people today find some aspects of Old Testament worship difficult to understand – especially sacrifice which (at least to Western people) seems primitive and cruel, if not completely incomprehensible.

Marcion's solution to all this was simple: tear up the Old Testament and throw it in the dustbin! But his view found no widespread support in the early church, not least because Marcion wanted to dispose of much of the New Testament as well, and that seemed to put a serious question mark against the reality of his Christian faith.

But the leaders of the early church could understand well enough the point that Marcion was making. There was a real question about the Old Testament. If the coming of Jesus was God's new and decisive action in the life of the world, then what relevance could the history of an ancient people have for faith in him?

The usual answer was that when the Old Testament was correctly understood it could be seen to be saying exactly the same thing as the New Testament. But in order to demonstrate this, it was necessary to interpret the Old Testament in such a way as to show that its real meaning was somehow hidden from the casual reader.

By coincidence, Jewish scholars had already faced this question in a different context. A century and more earlier, the great Jewish interpreter Philo (about 20 BC–AD 45), who lived in the Egyptian city of Alexandria, had taken up the challenge of reconciling the Old Testament with the thinking of the great Greek philosophers. There were few obvious connexions between them. But by applying a mystical allegorical interpretation to the Old Testament, Philo had succeeded in demonstrating (at least to his own satisfaction) that Moses and other Old Testament writers had actually declared the truths of Greek philosophy several centuries before the Greeks thought of them!

Some of the early Christian leaders, especially those in Alexandria, adopted this approach with enthusiasm. Soon, they were using the same techniques to show that the Old Testament books also contained everything that was in the New Testament, for those with the eyes to see it.

Even apparently insignificant details in the Old Testament stories were taken up as symbols of the Christian gospel. Anything red could be understood as a reference to the death of Jesus on the cross (for example, the

How far did Jesus set aside the Old Testament's detailed teachings? His disciples were criticized for picking and eating ears of wheat on a sabbath day.

red heifer of Numbers 19, or Rahab's red cord, Joshua 2:18). References to water soon became pictures of Christian baptism. The story of the exodus, with its combination of blood (on the doorposts at Passover) and water (in crossing the Sea of Reeds), engendered many complex explanations of the relationship between the cross and Christian salvation, as well as the two Christian sacraments of baptism and the Lord's Supper!

Hilary, bishop of Poitiers in France (AD 315–68), explained this way of reading the Old Testament in the following terms:

> Every work contained in the sacred volume announces by word, explains by facts, and corroborates by examples the coming of our Lord Jesus Christ ... From the beginning of the world Christ, by authentic and absolute prefigurations in the person of the patriarchs, gives birth to the church, washes it clean, sanctifies it, chooses it, places it apart and redeems it: by the sleep of Adam, by the deluge in the days of Noah, by the blessing of Melchizedek, by Abraham's justification, by the birth of Isaac, by the captivity of Jacob ... The purpose of this work is to show that in each personage in every age, and in every act, the image of his coming, of his teaching, of his resurrection, and of our church is reflected as in a mirror.
> (Hilary, Introduction to *The Treatise of Mysteries*)

Not all church leaders were happy with this approach to the Old Testament, especially those connected with the other great Christian centre at Antioch in Syria. But it was generally taken for granted that the Old Testament was basically a Christian book, and in one way or another its contents were related to the fundamental beliefs of Christian theology.

During the Protestant Reformation the whole subject was once again opened for fresh examination. Martin Luther (1483–1546) and John Calvin (1509–1564) both emphasized the need to understand the Old Testament faith in its historical and social context. In that respect their approach was not dissimilar from that of many modern scholars. But Luther wanted to distinguish the value of Old and New Testaments by seeing the Old as 'Law' and the New as 'Gospel'. This gave him a neat tool with which to separate out the wheat of the pure gospel (which for him was found in Paul's New Testament letters) from the chaff of a superseded legalism (identified with the Old Testament and Jewish Christianity). This thinking has had a profound influence on biblical scholarship right up to our own day. But it is misguided in some fundamental ways:

This 'Good Shepherd' is from a painting by Christians in the catacombs of Rome. The idea of God as a shepherd is taken straight from the Old Testament.

● It ignores the fact that 'law' is not the basis of the Old Testament faith – nor for that matter is it entirely absent from the New Testament. In both, law is placed in the context of a covenant understanding in which God's love is the foundation principle.

● Luther quite wrongly identified Judaism with a moralistic legalism. This was quite unfair even to the Pharisaic view which the Christian Paul so clearly rejected. At this point, Luther allowed

his own reaction to Roman Catholic Christianity to colour his view of the Old Testament faith.

Calvin recognized some of these deficiencies, and instead he emphasized the importance of the covenant theme in both Testaments. By a careful comparison of God's relationships with people in ancient Israel and the Christian church, he was able to claim that the two parts of the Christian Bible hang together as a kind of 'progressive

A Roman schoolmaster with his pupils. Paul writes in Galatians of the law as 'our tutor to bring us to Christ'.

In both Old and New Testaments the moral demands which stem from faith in God are carried right home to the daily life of ordinary people.

revelation' in which the ancient promises made to Israel in the Old Testament found their culmination in the ongoing life of the Christian church. This view is not without its own problems. But at least it does try to take the Old Testament faith seriously, and Calvin's position is still widely held today by many conservative Christians.

After the Reformation, the question of whether the Old Testament is a Christian book was effectively shelved until our own generation. The European Enlightenment, with its emphasis on understanding the Old Testament as a collection of ancient books in the context of its own times, directed scholarly endeavours elsewhere. But in the last 100 years or so, the theological question has again come to the fore. A significant impetus in this came from the Nazi movement in modern Germany. The anti-Jewish feelings that this created inevitably had repercussions in the German churches, and the presence of the Old Testament in the Christian Bible became a burning political issue as well as a subject for theological reflexion. A whole string of German theologians began to adopt the same kind of stance as Marcion. Yet despite the political pressures, many German Christian scholars made a positive assessment of the worth of the Old Testament. Some of the most creative work was done at this time by scholars such as Walter Eichrodt and Gerhard von Rad, as well as the Swiss theologian Karl Barth.

Nowadays, Christian people adopt various attitudes to the value of the Old Testament:

● Some would want to give the Old Testament an equal value and authority to the New Testament, on the grounds that every word of each is the direct utterance of God himself. But we need to exercise considerable caution before accepting this picture too easily. For there are whole sections of the teaching of Jesus himself where he makes it clear that his message involved either a rejection or a very radical revision of some fundamental aspects of Old Testament teaching.

● Others argue that the Old Testament is completely replaced by the New, and so can be discarded. Here again we need to preserve the kind of careful balance we find in the teaching of Jesus himself. For he also described his ministry as in some sense a 'fulfilment' of the Old Testament. We can legitimately argue about what that means – but it must certainly involve the assumption that the Old Testament has something to say to Christians, and therefore has a legitimate place in a Christian Bible.

● Some people try to distinguish between various parts of the Old Testament. They will separate things such as laws about priests, sacrifices, and purity (which Christians no longer observe) from other parts such as the Ten Commandments and the moral teachings of the prophets (which are still considered relevant). Calvin made a similar division to this. But it is a good deal easier to make such distinctions than it is to justify them. By removing such apparently irrelevant elements, we are in fact displacing some of the most basic aspects of the Old Testament faith. In addition, it is precisely in such concepts as sacrifice that the New Testament itself most often finds some correlation between the Old Testament faith and Christian beliefs about Jesus.

● It is also common for Christians to speak of a 'progressive revelation' of God's will and character running through both Testaments. On this view, God's will is revealed in a number of stages, roughly corresponding with the capacity of people to understand. So some of the more 'difficult' parts of the Old Testament can be explained as appropriate to a primitive age, but subsequently replaced by other more sophisticated notions, culminating in Jesus' teaching about a God of love. But this is an unhelpful idea. It is based on an outmoded evolutionary idea of an inevitable moral progress in human affairs. And it also confuses statements about God as he really is with statements about how people think of him. In addition, it contains the dubious implication that modern people invariably know more about God's will, and are more obedient to it than were the patriarchs, prophets and other leading figures in the Old Testament story.

Making connexions

There are obvious difficulties involved in interpreting the Old Testament within the Christian Bible. We need to recognize that the Old Testament is in many ways a strange and alien book to modern people – whether Christians or not. Whatever assessment we make of the Old Testament faith, it is not the same as Christian faith, and

in practice when Christians read it they often find the Old Testament hard to understand, because it belongs to a completely different world from their own faith experience. Much of this strangeness can be dispelled when once we have set the Old Testament faith in its proper historical and social context – and that is what we have tried to do here. We may not find things such as sacrifice any more appealing, but at least we can begin to appreciate their significance in the total context of Israel's faith. But that does not mean we can simply set the Old Testament on one side. For in practice it is impossible to articulate an adequate Christian faith without reference to the Old Testament.

At the most fundamental level, it is a simple fact that we will not get far in making sense out of the New Testament itself if we are ignorant of the Old. Jesus and his disciples were practising Jews. They were thoroughly immersed in Old Testament ways of thinking about God and the world. For them the Old Testament faith was a living and vital part of their total existence. Of course, in many respects they grew out of Judaism, as they found some things had to be discarded or developed in the light of the exciting newness of God's actions in Christ. But for all that they continued to think of their new Christian experience very much in terms of the faith with which they had been brought up.

The earliest Christian churches used the Old Testament in its Greek translation as their Bible – and the language of the New Testament itself has a good deal more in common with that than with the secular literature of Greek and Roman culture. Inevitably, that language influenced the way they articulated their understanding of Christianity. Indeed, Old Testament language still permeates Christian thinking today. Modern Western Christians who have never seen an animal sacrifice still sing in their churches of the 'one true, pure immortal sacrifice' of Jesus, and many of them continue to call a part of their church buildings an 'altar', even though no blood has ever been shed there! It may well be that we need to examine all this imagery and articulate its message in different concepts for modern people. But to do that successfully we need to understand it all first – otherwise we will be in constant danger of throwing out the fact that Christ died for our sins along with the language of sacrifice, altar and atonement. And the place where we can get a proper understanding of all these notions is certainly the Old Testament.

But the Old Testament gives us more than just a linguistic and cultural background to the thinking of the New Testament writers. It also contains important statements of truths about God and his relationships with people and the world that are as valid now as they ever were. If we take the chapter headings under which we have explored the Old Testament faith, we can readily see how the key concepts of each section form an indispensable theological foundation for the Christian faith as that is presented in the pages of the New Testament. There is such a close interconnexion between both Testaments at this point that it is no exaggeration to claim that the Christian faith itself would make imperfect sense if we were to remove the basic affirmations of the Old Testament faith from the Christian Bible.

The living God

Nowhere is this more strikingly obvious than in the case of beliefs about God himself.

● There is the truth that there is only one God, and that he is both all-powerful and yet personally interested in the welfare of ordinary people. Nowadays, theologians often talk of these two aspects of God's character in terms of 'transcendence' and 'immanence'. We can be quite sure that this language would have meant little to the people of Old Testament times. Indeed, it is unlikely that these truths about God would be perceived with equal clarity by all sections of the people of Israel. But they were certainly implicit in the very earliest creedal confessions which exhort the people to worship only one God – even if it was several centuries later that God's sole control of the world and its affairs was systematically asserted by the great prophets.

● Bound up with the fact that God is one is the belief that God's demands on his people are primarily moral rather than religious

Exodus 15:11–18

Isaiah 40:12–31; 41:21–29; 44:1–20

A shepherd leads his flock, just as God leads his people.

services or ritual taboos. We have already seen that this was a new idea, for most ancient religions were more interested in sacrifices and ritual than in morality. Yet the whole Old Testament understanding of worship makes no sense at all if these two aspects are separated.

● Then there is the notion of God's grace – the fact that he gives undeserved gifts to people. The entire Old Testament story is given coherence by the knowledge that God had done great things for his people, and on that basis he could challenge them to loyalty and obedience. Every stage of the story shows God's active concern to work for the salvation of his people – and this 'covenant' principle is still basic to any Christian understanding of God and his ways. The Old Testament, just as much as the New Testament, depicts God working in love for the good of his people. And though the focus in the New Testament shifts from events such as the exodus or the exile to centre on Jesus, there is still a basic assumption that God is an active and loving God, whose workings can be seen by ordinary people in the course of their everyday lives.

● We have observed at a number of points that the Old Testament does not describe God 'metaphysically', by asking what he is made of, but 'functionally', by asking how he behaves. The New Testament shares this approach, when it says in effect: 'Look at Jesus: this is what God is like.'

God and the world

It is not too difficult to show that important aspects of God's character are common to both Testaments. But without the Old Testament, the Christian faith would also be seriously lacking a perspective on the way God relates to the natural world.

● In the world of the earliest Christians, it was commonplace to believe that the natural, physical world in which we live was intrinsically evil, and any sort of meaningful salvation would therefore need to involve an escape from this world to some other, more 'spiritual' and therefore more perfect world. This was part and parcel of the Greek outlook, and as the Christian church moved out from Palestine into the wider Roman Empire it was always a temptation for Christians to agree with it. Though there were fierce arguments on this very point, Christians never did accept the view that physical existence in this world is second best. But they were able to assert the basic goodness of life only because of the strong Old Testament conviction that informed their thinking. As a consequence, instead of seeing salvation in terms of escape from this world, the Christian writers of the New Testament declared that the world itself had its own part in God's plan of salvation: the coming of Jesus meant vitality and renewal for the very stuff out of which the world is made. Without this, modern Christians would have little to say on the major issues of the twentieth century, such as the nuclear arms race or the use of the world's resources. But in taking the physical world into their expectations of salvation, the New Testament writers were quite firmly grounded in the Old Testament faith that had gone before them.

Romans 8:18–25; Colossians 1:15–20; Revelation 21 — 22

● When the New Testament sets out to explain how Jesus Christ relates to people, it again does so on the basis of the Old Testament view of people and their relationship to God. It takes for granted the basic theological concepts that we have located in the creation stories, and sees human sin as a barrier between God and people that needs to be removed if fellowship is to be restored. This whole structure of thought is so crucial for Christian theology that without this Old Testament insight it is doubtful whether the apostolic faith could have developed in the way it did.

God and his people

New Testament ethics also owe a good deal to the Old Testament.

● The notion of 'natural law' as we have discussed it in relation to the Old Testament is a fundamental prerequisite of the Christian faith. Paul takes it up as a key element in his explanation of how the life, death and resurrection of Jesus applies to all men and women, whatever their social or racial origins.

Romans 1:18 — 2:16

● Equally central to the New Testament is the covenant framework within which much Old Testament morality operates. The coming of Jesus was viewed as a further great act of God comparable with the exodus, and calling for a similar response of obedience and commitment. But the whole pattern of the Christian ethic is also based on the fundamental Old Testament assertion that people should behave like God behaves. The only difference is that the divine pattern is made even more explicit because of the example of Jesus himself, which Christians are called on to follow.

Matthew 5:48

Philippians 2:5–11; 2 Corinthians 8:8–9

● Then there is also the whole question of a Christian social ethic, which depends so much on the Old Testament heritage. For a variety of reasons, the New Testament has very little to say about how God deals with nations. Without the Old Testament, the Christian faith would be considerably impoverished at this point. For in the Old Testament faith we have the foundations of a Christian philosophy of history. No doubt the Old Testament position requires modification here and there in the light of the teaching of Jesus himself. But it is no coincidence that when modern Christians make pronouncements on social and political affairs they so often depend on the insights of the prophets and lawgivers of ancient Israel as they do so.

Worshipping God

Here too, the New Testament faith owes more than we sometimes think to its Old Testament antecedents.

● The style of worship of the early church – and of many modern churches – has grown out of the patterns of praise and joyful celebration that we have seen in the pages of the Old Testament.

● Even more striking is the correlation between the understanding of what worship means in both Testaments. For the undergirding principle of both Old Testament and Christian worship is that although God is a holy God – in every sense of that word – he is also a forgiving God, and the reality of that forgiveness can be represented in the events of worship in the presence of God's people.

● We can hardly ignore the vast importance that the theme of sacrifice has come to assume in Christian thinking. The New Testament writers asserted that in Jesus' life, death and resurrection, all that was promised by the sacrificial worship of the Old Testament had been brought to fulfilment. It was impossible to speak of what Jesus could do in the lives of his people without some reference to the hopes and aspirations of the worshipper in ancient Israel. Indeed, the whole concept of sacrifice is so significant in the Christian tradition that at least one large section of the church thinks of it not only as a series of theological metaphors and images, but as a continuing symbolic part of the ongoing liturgy of the worshipping Christian community.

Looking to the future

No one will wish to dispute the reality of the various connexions we have traced here between the Old Testament faith and its New Testament development. Indeed, much more could be said along these lines which would reinforce the general picture presented here. But is all this just wishful thinking from the Christian's point of view? After all, it is easy enough to look at the Old Testament with the benefit of hindsight and convince oneself that this or that element of Old Testament faith is somehow related to Christian thinking. Are we perhaps in danger of falling into the same kind of subjectivism as those more ancient expositors who looked at things such as Rahab's scarlet cord and saw in them a clear reference to the blood of Jesus on the cross?

We are certainly not in the same predicament as the medieval scholars, for we have restricted our discussion here to features in the Old Testament faith which were an integral part of its historical development, and which were clearly perceived by the Old Testament writers themselves. But we still need to explain how we can be so sure that the Christian interpretation we want to place on these facts is not an alien intrusion into the Old Testament's essential message.

In the final analysis, of course, it is only our Christian conviction that Jesus is God's final word that enables us to see both Old and New Testaments as parts of the same story. But we could certainly qualify that by observing the simple fact that the Old Testament writers did see their faith as incomplete in itself, and therefore requiring some future 'fulfilment'.

In many important respects, the Old Testament faith was anchored in the past. Some of its most distinctive insights emerged out of the great events of Israel's history. When men and women wanted to know what God was like, they turned for an answer to events such as the exodus or the exile, as explained by the prophets and others. But they never thought that God was locked up in the past. Quite the opposite, in fact. For one of the Old Testament's fundamental convictions is that God can be known by ordinary people in the everyday events of their present life. The prophets extended these beliefs to their logical conclusion, observing that if

God was the Lord of the past, and if he also made himself known in the present, then he must be Lord of the future too.

The Old Testament historians express this view right at the beginning of their long story. For when God makes a covenant with Abraham and his family, he does so in the following terms: 'I will bless those who bless you, but I will curse those who curse you. *And through you I will bless all the nations.*'

Genesis 12:3

There is some debate as to the precise meaning of that last phrase. But it is certain that this blessing of the nations was not a reality at the time the Old Testament was compiled: it was a future hope that had yet to be accomplished.

As the Old Testament story proceeds, this hope is expanded and combined with other themes until a coherent future expectation emerges. This forward look to the Old Testament faith is so strong that Gerhard von Rad has described the Old Testament as a whole as 'a book of ever increasing anticipation'. We may trace at least three fundamental strands in this.

● **A new covenant** Perhaps the most notable is the expectation of a 'new covenant', that would take up and fulfil all the broken promises of the original Sinai covenant, and at the same time herald the beginning of a new era of relationships between God and people. This hope first emerged about the time of the exile, when it was clear that the original covenant had been a failure because of the disobedience and disloyalty of the people. For all its God-given

Promise and fulfilment

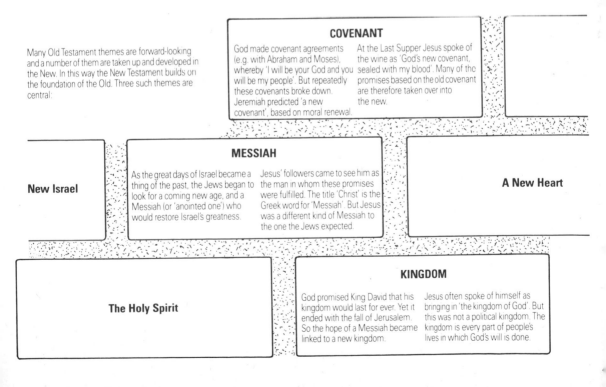

Many Old Testament themes are forward-looking and a number of them are taken up and developed in the New. In this way the New Testament builds on the foundation of the Old. Three such themes are central:

COVENANT

God made covenant agreements (e.g. with Abraham and Moses), whereby 'I will be your God and you will be my people'. But repeatedly these covenants broke down. Jeremiah predicted 'a new covenant', based on moral renewal.

At the Last Supper Jesus spoke of the wine as 'God's new covenant, sealed with my blood'. Many of the promises based on the old covenant are therefore taken over into the new.

New Israel

MESSIAH

As the great days of Israel became a thing of the past, the Jews began to look for a coming new age, and a Messiah (or 'anointed one') who would restore Israel's greatness.

Jesus' followers came to see him as the man in whom these promises were fulfilled. The title 'Christ' is the Greek word for 'Messiah'. But Jesus was a different kind of Messiah to the one the Jews expected.

A New Heart

The Holy Spirit

KINGDOM

God promised King David that his kingdom would last for ever. Yet it ended with the fall of Jerusalem. So the hope of a Messiah became linked to a new kingdom.

Jesus often spoke of himself as bringing in 'the kingdom of God'. But this was not a political kingdom. The kingdom is every part of people's lives in which God's will is done.

potential, they had been unable to keep its terms. As a result, leading Old Testament thinkers began to see that a complete change was needed in the lives of God's people if ever they were to do God's will. This change would be based on forgiveness for what was past. But its most striking feature would be a radical transformation of the human will in such a way that God would empower his people actually to keep the covenant. 'The new covenant that I will make with the people of Israel will be this: I will put my law within them and write it on their hearts.' The key to success is found in the new initiative from God himself to enable people to do his will: 'I will give you a new heart and a new mind. I will take away your stubborn heart of stone and give you an obedient heart. I will put my spirit in you ...'

Jeremiah 31:33

Ezekiel 36:26–27; 11:19–20

● **A Messiah** The Hebrew word *Mashiach*, like its Greek equivalent *Christos*, means 'an anointed person'. In the ancient Middle East both kings and priests were anointed with oil. We have already noticed the important part played by the king in so much of Old Testament life, especially in the southern kingdom of Judah. As the representative of God to his people, he was often referred to as 'God's anointed', even as 'God's Son'. This close relationship between God and the king in Jerusalem was cemented in the covenant made with the royal family of David. Because of that, the king was in a very real sense the focus of the people's hopes as they looked for God's will to be done in their midst.

Psalm 2:7

2 Samuel 7:1–17

If Old Testament social relationships were to reflect the character of God himself, then it was through the king that this would be put into practical effect. At least, that was the theory. But the reality was often different, as one king after another showed himself to be quite unfit, both morally and spiritually, to lead his people in ways that would reflect God's standards. Not that this prevented the prophets and others from hoping that the next king would be better. But from about the time of Isaiah onwards they were to become increasingly disillusioned with David's family. Though the prophets greeted each new king with optimism, their hopes for the future came to be expressed in more idealistic terms that show their expectations moving away from the actual kings in Jerusalem and towards an ideal king whom God himself would send to lead his people. It was out of this frustration that the messianic hope eventually was born. By the end of the Old Testament period it was widely believed that God would once more intervene in history, and send a new king who would perfectly fulfil the hopes and aspirations of the ancient Old Testament faith.

Psalm 72:1–19

Isaiah 9:6–7; 11:1–5; Micah 5:2–5; Jeremiah 23:5–6; Psalm 89:1–4; 132:10–12

● **A new world** The Old Testament also looks forward to a time of physical renewal for the world itself. It often links failure in the lives of people with corruption in the world of nature. So it is not surprising that future personal and social renewal should also include plans for a revitalized world. This, too, became an important part of the Old Testament view of the future, and many passages depict the material world sharing in the rejuvenation of the human world.

Genesis 3:17–19; Amos 4:6–12

Isaiah 11:6–9; 25:6–9; 51:3; 62:1–5; Amos 9:13–15; Micah 4:1–4; Ezekiel 47:1–12

Nowhere in the Bible is the believer thought to have arrived at moral perfection. Paul, in his letter to the Philippians, takes an image from the chariot races and writes of 'pressing on' to reach that goal.

The Old Testament faith is not a closed system, but a dynamic living faith that always expects God to do new things. This message is given its most comprehensive form by one of the later Old Testament prophets. As he sought to encourage the exiles, Isaiah of Babylon told them to direct their attention away from sentimental assessments of the past, and to look for God to do new things in their midst. He knew they could trust God not only because of his past deeds on their behalf but also because he was 'the first, the last, the only God; there is no other god but me'. He also identified God's action on behalf of his people with the work of a figure he called 'the servant of Yahweh'.

Isaiah 43:18–19

Isaiah 44:6

It is customary in Old Testament studies to refer to four 'servant songs' which describe the work of this person. One scholar has recently suggested that these 'songs' are not in fact such distinct literary entities as has generally been supposed. But there can be no doubt that 'the servant' had an important place in the prophet's message. For he is portrayed as one who fulfils in his own life and experience all those aspects of God's will that Israel as a nation had been unable to accomplish.

Isaiah 42:1–4; 49:1–6; 50:4–9; 52:13 — 53:12

Jewish readers of the Old Testament never identified this figure with the Messiah. That was natural, for one of the distinctive features of the servant poems is that he was to be a *suffering* servant – and the Messiah was always thought of as an all-powerful conquering king. But it was this very feature of the servant's work that led the early Christians to see here an expectation that had been fulfilled in Jesus himself. For especially in the final servant passage, we find two themes that correlate very closely with the facts of Jesus' own life: the servant, though innocent, suffers for the wrongdoings of other people; and following that, God will vindicate the servant in such a way that the great and powerful will be astonished while those for whom he suffers will realize he has suffered in their place.

Isaiah 53:4–9

Isaiah 53:10–12

Writing of this aspect of the Old Testament's forward look, Professor G. W. Anderson has commented: 'in spite of all uncertainties of interpretation, the anticipation in the fourth song of the Passion of Christ is one of the miracles of Old Testament literature.' For Christians, it is perhaps the one theme that helps them to see the continuity between Old and New. At the same time they recognize that the two Testaments are distinctive in their own right.

Many efforts have been made to identify the consistency of the Christian Bible. Terms such as the covenant, or the idea of 'salvation history' have been suggested as the cement which binds together such apparently discordant literature into one coherent block. But perhaps the only real continuity in the midst of such diversity and discontinuity is God himself.

God constantly occupies the centre of the stage – searching for people, making new relationships with them, and motivated only by his own generous love. God himself is the unifying factor in the message of both Old and New. From beginning to end, he is engaged in the establishment of order out of the chaos which so easily engulfs the life of society and of the physical world, as well as the personal experience of individuals. For Christians, that process culminated in the life, death and resurrection of Jesus, and the gift of the Holy Spirit at Pentecost. It is in this sense that both Testaments bear witness to him: 'Christ is given to us only through the double witness of the choir of those who await and those who remember.'

Gerhard von Rad

Other books on the Old Testament

There are very many books on Old
Testament theology and the history of
Old Testament religion. This list is
limited to those which would be readily
accessible to the general reader, though
one or two of them are more advanced
and are marked with an asterisk(*). The
books listed in *The Old Testament Story*
may also be relevant to some aspects of
the Old Testament faith.

Chapter One. Defining the faith

* G. W. Anderson (ed.), *Tradition and
Interpretation*, OUP 1979. Essays by
leading Old Testament scholars,
surveying the present opinions on
various aspects of Old Testament
literature.

R. E. Clements, *Old Testament
Theology*, Marshall, Morgan & Scott,
1978/John Knox Press, 1980. An
attempt to define what we mean by 'Old
Testament theology', together with an
account of some of the important issues
raised by it.

R. Davidson, *The Old Testament*,
Hodder & Stoughton/Lippincott, 1964.
A helpful elementary introduction to
the various strands that go to make up
the Old Testament faith.

*W. Eichrodt, *The Theology of the Old
Testament*, 2 vols, SCM Press/
Westminster Press, 1961 & 1967. An
encyclopedic exposition of the subject,
trying to use the idea of 'covenant' as
the central theme of the Old
Testament.

*G. Fohrer, *History of Israelite Religion*,
Abingdon Press, 1972/SPCK, 1973.
The best historical account of the
development of Israel's religious history
and institutions.

J. Goldingay, *Approaches to Old
Testament Interpretation*, IVP,
1981/Inter-Varsity (USA) 1982. A
readable account of the state of play
among Old Testament experts on many
aspects of the subject.

* G. Hasel, *Old Testament Theology:
basic issues in the current debate*,
Eerdmans, 1975 (2nd ed.). A judicious
appraisal of the present position of Old
Testament scholarship.

E. Jacob, *Theology of the Old Testament*,
Hodder & Stoughton/Harper & Row,
1958.

* G. Von Rad, *Old Testament Theology*,
2 vols, Oliver & Boyd/Harper & Row,
1962 & 1965. One of the classic Old
Testament theologies, trying to
establish 'salvation history' as the centre
of the Old Testament faith.

J. Rogerson (ed.), *Beginning Old
Testament Study*, Westminster
Press/SPCK, 1983. A helpful
introductory book, setting out clearly
and simply the various ways in which we
can read and interpret the Old
Testament.

H. H. Rowley, *The Faith of Israel*, SCM
Press, 1956/Westminster Press, 1957. A
generally enlightening attempt to distil
some elements of a 'systematic
theology' from the Old Testament.

*W. H. Schmidt, *The Faith of the Old
Testament*, Westminster Press/
Blackwell,1983/ Not quite an Old
Testament theology, but more than just
a 'history of religion' – though it is set
out historically.

*W. Zimmerli, *Old Testament Theology
in Outline*, John Knox Press, 1978. A
systematic and scholarly treatment of its
subject.

Chapter Two. The living God

D. Baly, *God and History in the Old
Testament*, Harper and Row, 1976.
Almost a comprehensive Old
Testament theology, but with a
particular concern to grasp what the
Old Testament means by the term
'God'.

*R. C. Dentan, *The Knowledge of God in
Ancient Israel*, Seabury Press, 1968.

R. Davidson, *The Courage to Doubt*,
SCM Press, 1983. A valuable and
comprehensive study of the
'hiddenness' of God in the Old
Testament.

R. Gordis, *The Book of God and Man*,
University of Chicago Press, 1965. A
comprehensive exposition of the book
of Job.

*G. H. Parke-Taylor, *Yahweh: the
Divine Name in the Bible*, Wilfrid
Laurier University Press, 1975. An
exhaustive but readable account.

N. H. Snaith, *The Distinctive Ideas of the
Old Testament*, Epworth Press, 1944.
Detailed study of a number of key
themes used to describe God.

N. H. Snaith, *The Book of Job*, SCM
Press, 1968. A helpful survey of the
possible ways the book of Job can be
interpreted.

C. Westermann, *What does the Old
Testament say about God?* John Knox
Press/SPCK, 1979. A first-rate book by
an eminent German scholar.

Chapter Three. God and the world

B. W. Anderson (ed.), *Creation in the Old Testament,* Fortress Press/SPCK, 1984. A collection of essays (some of them classics) on various aspects of the creation theme.

R. Davidson, *Genesis 1–11,* CUP, 1973 (The Cambridge Bible Commentaries). A straightforward and helpful exposition.

D. Kidner, *Genesis,* IVP, 1967/Inter-Varsity (USA) 1968 (The Tyndale Old Testament Commentaries). Tries to reconcile Genesis and science, linking the Genesis creation stories with evolutionary thinking.

F. R. McCurley, *Ancient Myths and Biblical Faith,* Fortress Press 1983. A brief account of the relationships between some biblical materials and comparative ancient literature.

H. McKeating, *Why bother with Adam and Eve?* Lutterworth Press, 1982. A readable and illuminating answer to the question, setting it in the broader context of belief.

* J. W.Rogerson, *Myth in Old Testament Interpretation,* De Gruyter, 1974. A comprehensive and helpful exploration of the whole concept of 'myth', as related to many themes in Old Testament thinking.

Chapter Four. God and his people

*A. Alt, *Essays on Old Testament History and Religion,* Blackwell, 1966/Doubleday, 1967. Contains the essay on Old Testament laws referred to in our discussion.

J. Blenkinsopp, *Wisdom and Law in the Old Testament,* OUP, 1983. A valuable study of the relationship between these two strands of Old Testament morality.

J. L. Crenshaw, *Old Testament Wisdom,* John Knox Press, 1981/SCM Press, 1982. The most useful recent general introduction to the world of the wisdom teachers.

W. Harrelson, *The Ten Commandments and Human Rights,* Fortress Press 1980. Considers all the issues of interpretation and meaning raised by the Ten Commandments – historical, as well as theological and contemporary.

* A.Phillips, *Ancient Israel's Criminal Law,* Blackwell, 1970. The study referred to in our discussion.

* J. W. Rogerson, *Anthropology and the Old Testament,* Blackwell, 1978. An interesting study of clan structures in ancient Israel, including useful discussions of questions relating to responsibility and corporate personality.

R. de Vaux, *Ancient Israel,* McGraw-Hill/Darton, Longman & Todd, 1965 (2nd ed.). A helpful discussion of the administration of justice, pages 143-77.

C. J. H. Wright, *Living as the People of God,* IVP, 1983. The first new book on Old Testament ethics for almost 50 years. Especially good on social ethics.

Chapter Five. Worshipping God

M.F.C. Bourdillon & M. Fortes, *Sacrifice,* Academic Press, 1980. An interesting and helpful study by both anthropologists and theologians. Technical in places – but well worth persevering with.

J. H. Hayes, *Understanding the Psalms,* Judson Press, 1976. A simple general introduction to its subject.

H. Ringgren, *Israelite Religion,* Fortress Press/SPCK, 1966. Good on worship, priesthood, and related matters, especially pages 151-219.

H. H. Rowley, *Worship in Ancient Israel,* Fortress Press/SPCK, 1967. A comprehensive and balanced study of the subject, dealing with it both historically and topically and covering the whole of the Old Testament period.

L. Sabourin, *The Psalms: their origin and meaning,* Alba House, 1974. One of the most comprehensive surveys of current thinking on the psalms and their place in worship.

R. de Vaux, *Ancient Israel,* especially pages 271-517.

Chapter Six. The Old and the New

D. L. Baker, *Two Testaments, One Bible*, IVP, 1976. An exhaustive survey of modern attempts to find a single theological unity between Old and New Testaments.

J. Barr, *Old and New in Interpretation*, SCM Press/Harper & Row, 1982 (2nd ed.). An incisive study of the issues involved, with many helpful insights.

*J. Becker, *Messianic Expectation in the Old Testament*, Fortress Press/T & T Clark, 1980. An account of selected aspects of the subject.

J. Bright, *The Authority of the Old Testament*, Abingdon Press/SCM Press, 1967 (subsequently reprinted by Baker Book House). Essential reading on the problems of using the Old Testament in the Christian church. Faces all the most difficult questions head-on, and makes many helpful practical suggestions.

A. G. Hebert, *The Authority of the Old Testament*, Faber, 1947. An older examination of the subject, though still valuable for its historical and analytical approach.

* S. M. Mayo, *The Relevance of the Old Testament for the Christian Faith*, University Press of America, 1982.

D. G. Miller, *The Authority of the Bible*, Eerdmans, 1972. Contains a useful chapter on the place of the Old Testament in the Christian Bible.

*S. Mowinckel, *He That Cometh*, Abingdon Press/Blackwell, 1956. An encyclopedic study of the Messianic hope, from its beginnings through to New Testament times.

Index